D1552637

INTERNATIONAL TRANSFER PRICING POLICIES

INTERNATIONAL TRANSFER PRICING POLICIES

Decision-Making Guidelines for Multinational Companies

WAGDY M. ABDALLAH

QUORUM BOOKS

New York • Westport, Connecticut • London

658.816
A13i

Library of Congress Cataloging-in-Publication Data

Abdallah, Wagdy M. (Wagdy Moustafa)
International transfer pricing policies : decisionmaking
guidelines for multinational companies / Wagdy M. Abdallah.
p. cm.
Bibliography: p.
Includes index.
ISBN 0-89930-294-7 (lib. bdg. : alk. paper)
1. International business enterprises—Management.
2. Transfer pricing. I. Title.
HD62.45.A24 1989
658.8'16—dc 19   88-25258

British Library Cataloguing in Publication Data is available.

Library of Congress Catalog Card Number: 88-25258
ISBN: 0-89930-294-7

First published in 1989 by Quorum Books

Greenwood Press, Inc.
88 Post Road West, Westport, Connecticut 06881

Printed in the United States of America

The paper used in this book complies with the
Permanent Paper Standard issued by the National
Information Standards Organization (Z39.48-1984).

10 9 8 7 6 5 4 3 2 1

Contents

Exhibits

INTERNATIONAL TRANSFER PRICING POLICIES

1

Introduction

Multinational enterprises (MNEs) are motivated to go across the border of their home country by many factors that are different from one industry to another and even from one firm to another within the same industry. They may export to or import from a subsidiary in the foreign country owned by another MNE. In this case, a MNE, American or non-American, may manufacture its products at home and then export them to a foreign market and achieve higher profits. On the other hand, a MNE may find it cheaper to manufacture its products where labor costs are the lowest and sell them where selling prices are the highest.

MNEs may start to look for new markets outside their home country for many reasons. These reasons include (*a*) improving their competitive position in both domestic and international markets, (*b*) exploring new markets, (*c*) maximizing profits, (*d*) meeting tariff and quota restrictions in foreign countries, (*e*) securing otherwise unobtainable raw materials for the home country, (*f*) exploring the scarce economic resources in the third world countries, (*g*) choosing countries with low tariff and quota restrictions, (*h*) choosing countries with low income taxes on foreign companies or foreign investments, and (*i*) manufacturing their products in the least cost-producing countries, especially the less developed countries (LDCs), and selling the products in the best selling markets. However, foreign governments, especially of the third world countries, may impose very high tariffs on all imports getting into their countries either to protect their local industries from the competition against the foreign companies or to increase revenues for the government.

The growth of MNEs has created new issues for foreign national economies as well as international economies. These include international location of production and distribution territories, their effect on national and international stock and commodity markets, their significant effects on both home and host governments' revenues, and the balance of payments of both foreign and home countries.

However, to maximize profits, a MNE should produce in the least cost-producing countries and sell in the best market countries. To achieve this, top management must have an attitude of globalism that makes it as concerned and involved with each of its foreign operations around the world as with home-country operations, and that makes it attempt to rationalize and manage its operations on a global rather than a domestic basis within the constraints of its social, economic, political, legal, and educational conditions.[1] Consequently, the production and marketing operations in all foreign countries are integrated and coordinated on a global basis within the host and home national governments' restrictions.

One of the major characteristics of a successful MNE is having a highly efficient organizational tool for utilizing scarce economic resources on a worldwide basis. Moreover, if the headquarters at the home office is to achieve the goals set out in the strategic plan, the international activities of all its foreign and domestic subsidiaries need to be planned, organized, coordinated, and controlled on a global basis.

GLOBAL PLANNING AND GLOBAL ORGANIZATION

Top management, under global planning, is concerned with two major factors: (1) looking for the most effective method to localize its resources in order to take advantage of the efficiencies gained from the specialization of labor in different countries, and (2) coordinating the enterprise's activities to help to achieve its global objectives. Global planning can be done in two different ways by MNEs: centralized planning or decentralized planning.

A MNE's domestic and international activities, under global organization, may be divided into several separate groups or divisions. The authority for decision making is delegated to each group or division manager, who, in turn, coordinates the activities under his or her area of responsibility. The extent of decentralization or centralization of the decision-making process will specify the responsibility area of each manager.

A MNE may group its global activities in many different ways. It can be organized (a) on a functional basis, (b) on the basis of the product, or (c) on the basis of the geographical area. A global functional organization combines different activities by type, such as manufacturing, marketing, or finance. Each division manager is delegated the authority for decision making and coordinates the MNE's global manufacturing, marketing, or financing activities. Each area of responsibility may be treated as cost, profit, revenue, or investment center.

Under a global product organization approach, a MNE puts together manufacturing, marketing, and financing activities for each of its major products or groups of related products on a global basis into separate divisions for worldwide activities. In this case, each division is treated as a profit center, and the responsibility of each product's division manager is to coordinate the operating decisions for manufacturing, marketing, and financing the product for all domestic and international markets. Consequently, each manager usually tries to maximize his divisional profits, which are used as a basis for his accountability and over which he is presumed to have complete control.

Under geographical global organization, a MNE separates its activities into different geographic area divisions. Each geographic area manager is responsible for coordinating all activities under his control; therefore, he is delegated authority for divisional decision making. The firm may be divided into two main divisions, domestic and international. While the international division manager makes all decisions related to business outside the United States, the domestic division manager is responsible for all business activities inside the home country. On the other hand, the international division can be subdivided into different groups such as Europe, South America, North America, Middle East, and Far East by considering each group as one profit center.

GLOBAL CONTROL AND DECISION MAKING

Another important aspect under globalization is control or global control. Control, in general, is defined as "the process of ensuring that the organization is adapted to its environment and is pursuing courses of action that will enable it to achieve its purposes."[2] For a MNE with global control, top management is expected to globally coordinate and integrate its worldwide activities by putting its global plans into effect, to compare actual global results with its global plans, and to make whatever corrective actions are needed under the given environmental circumstances.

A fact not to be ignored is that a multinational environment is completely different from and more complicated than the U.S. environment, which means that careful coordination of international operations within the environmental factors involved is required before an adequate and appropriate control system is adopted. These environmental factors include different customs, languages, taxes, currencies, educational systems, capital markets, and political factors, among many others.

As a MNE grows and its international activities become larger and more complicated, it faces three problems: (1) how to assign responsibility and delegate authority to managers, (2) how much to decentralize or how many cost, revenue, profit, or investment centers to have and at what level to make decisions, and (3) how to coordinate and integrate its worldwide operations of all its subsidiaries. The growth of MNEs forces the headquarters in the home country to delegate decision authority. The manager then usually accepts the assigned authority to perform his job by making the necessary divisional decisions. Every organizational unit can be either cost, revenue, profit, or investment center. Since the organizational structure of a MNE must provide an effective decision-making process and a smooth flow of communications between various levels, groups, or individuals of the enterprise, it is necessary to give each manager of a subunit some authority to exercise control over certain kinds of activities.

GLOBAL CENTRALIZATION VERSUS DECENTRALIZATION

The issue of decentralization or centralization is critical because all other organizational forms are affected by the extent to which managerial decisions are or can be centralized. Centralization refers to the extent to which a manager is delegated the authority for decision making. A MNE is highly centralized when most decisions are made at the top management's levels and controls are somewhat strict throughout all levels. Decentralization refers to a decision-making process that gives the manager more freedom to make divisional decisions and implies a certain degree of autonomy.

In the area of international business, there are good points both for and against centralization. Under centralization, a MNE has relatively tight controls over all domestic and international operations. In addition, all strategic and operating decisions can be made by using the overall corporate resources within its global objectives.

On the other hand, individual managers of decentralized MNEs are given the authority to make decisions. Therefore, they must be held responsible for what they have control over and consequently for the results of their divisional decisions. Each subsidiary manager, domestic or foreign, can make his decisions on a more timely basis because he is the one most aware of the business environment and can make decisions relevant to the problems that arise in his subsidiary's local environment. Under these circumstances, foreign and domestic subsidiary managers are motivated to make the optimum divisional decisions to maximize their own divisional profits.

However, the best way to achieve a global strategy is for the corporate management team to determine its global objectives, to provide guidelines for worldwide organizational strategies and policies, to decide how to allocate economic resources, and to implement effective communication, coordination, integration, and control systems. Within these guidelines, foreign and domestic subsidiary managers are expected to make their own decisions with more freedom to achieve their subunit profits and at the same time the global profits of the MNE as a whole.[3]

The difference between centralization and decentralization is the extent to which top management delegates authority for managers to make both strategic and operating decisions, delegates authority for managers to make operating decisions only, or keeps both strategic and operating decisions at the top level of management. With a high degree of decentralization, a foreign or domestic subsidiary manager has authority to make most of the decisions related to his business. He decides what product is needed for the national market based on the expected demand, at what price to sell the product to the customers or to other subsidiaries of the same MNE, what equipment is needed, what materials to buy, and from where to buy. The outcome is to hold the manager accountable for the consequences of the decisions he made. Usually profits would be one of the indicators of his performance. Higher profits this year than last year, or than what was expected, would show a better performance, and lower profits a worse performance.

One of the major problems with a high degree of decentralization is that a manager may attempt to maximize his own division's profits at the expense of other divisions' profits, which would result in suboptimization in decision making and consequently in failure to maximize the global profits of the MNE as a whole. In addition, with a high degree of centralization, the corporate management wants to integrate and coordinate all international and domestic operations. In this case, top management has stronger control over all units. The corporate management does its best to bring the company's resources within control as efficiently as possible and to achieve the optimum utilization of these resources. In general, centralization versus decentralization is not a clear-cut issue. There are degrees of decentralization. The major issue is to determine which decisions should be decentralized and the extent to which they should be decentralized.

Practical examples of decentralization versus centralization can be illustrated by looking at the Charles Pfizer company as compared to international oil companies. Pfizer delegates more authority and consequently gives more autonomy to its subsidiary managers in decision making within the local environment within which the subsidiary operates. On the other hand, the international oil companies are less decentralized and maintain tight central control over the major functions such as production, finance, and marketing.[4]

In a decentralized MNE the profit-center concept has been used as the main basis of performance evaluation. A domestic or foreign subsidiary manager under this concept makes the major decisions relating to profit-center costs and revenues. Since he is able to influence the results of operations, he is accountable for and evaluated on the basis of these results, which are the profits of the profit center. The adoption of decentralized organization systems brings new problems for MNEs when they attempt to coordinate production decisions between domestic and foreign subsidiaries if production is done domestically and marketing is done internationally or vice versa, or among foreign subsidiaries when both production and marketing are done overseas.

THE INTERNATIONAL TRANSFER PRICING DILEMMA

One of the most important and complex considerations in coordinating and integrating production and marketing strategies is that of intracompany pricing. Should the product be transferred among a company's own subsidiaries at the world market price, and should each manager be given freedom in making his production and marketing decisions and consequently in maximizing his own profits? Do we assume that the market price will lead domestic and foreign subsidiaries to make production and marketing decisions in the best interest of the MNE as a whole? Or should full costs, variable costs, cost plus a percentage for markup, marginal costs of production, or marginal costs plus opportunity costs when there is no intermediate market for the product be used to determine the appropriate transfer price?

MNEs are usually organized into different subsidiaries whose managers are allowed considerable autonomy in day-to-day decision making. Each subsidiary transfers goods to others that are located in different countries under different political, legal, taxation, and governmental systems. The prices at which these goods are transferred affect subsidiary managers in making their divisional decisions, and some decisions may achieve divisional profits in the short run at the expense of the global profits in the long run when factors such as transportation costs, taxes paid to either home- or host-country governments, import duties, cash movement restrictions, or governmental rules, among others, are ignored.

Making pricing decisions for MNEs' products, in general, is an important, complex, flexible, and complicated task because these decisions affect other major functions of MNEs such as marketing, production location, transportation, and finance that directly affect its total sales and profits. Moreover, there is no clear-cut or easy way to establish an effective pricing policy. MNEs cannot just add a standard percentage as a markup to a full, variable, or marginal cost to come up with a price that they have to charge for goods sold externally or transferred internally among their own subsidiaries. However, if a pricing policy or decision can be considered as a controllable factor for MNE management, prices can go up or down to achieve certain objectives.[5]

A transfer price is defined as the price charged by a selling department, division, or subsidiary of a MNE for a product or service supplied to a buying department, division, or subsidiary of the same MNE. For all domestic operations of MNEs, intracompany transfers of goods or services can be determined by one of the traditional techniques: (*a*) full actual cost method, (*b*) full standard cost,

(c) actual variable cost, (*d*) standard variable cost, (*e*) cost plus, (*f*) market price method, or (*g*) negotiated price. Under the cost method, the transfer price can be determined on the basis of actual or standard full costs, actual or standard variable costs, or variable or fixed costs plus a fixed amount or a percentage of cost.

Under the market price method, the transfer price is the price at which significant quantities of goods and services are generally sold to third parties who are external to the firm and dealing at arm's length with one another. A negotiated transfer price is determined by bargaining between buyer and seller subsidiaries, presuming that both subunits have freedom or equal power or authority to bargain.

The choice of the appropriate technique for transfer pricing should be based on the following four criteria: (*a*) how well it promotes goal congruence and consequently profit maximization, (*b*) how well it provides an adequate profit yardstick for performance evaluation of subsidiaries and their managers, (*c*) how well it guides top management in making decisions, and (*d*) how well it promotes more autonomy for divisional or subsidiary managers in decision making.[6]

MNEs face a major problem as they transfer goods and services between their subsidiaries, that of deciding at what price to transfer goods and services among their foreign subsidiaries or between the parent and its foreign subsidiaries. The 1972 Committee on International Accounting of the American Accounting Association indicated that the lack of an approach to transfer pricing that is compatible with the objectives of MNEs is one of the troublesome techniques preventing MNEs from moving toward global coordination and integration for their worldwide business operations.[7]

FACTORS AFFECTING INTERNATIONAL TRANSFER PRICING POLICIES

International transfer pricing of a MNE is the process of setting prices for intracompany transactions when the buying subsidiary is in a different country from the selling subsidiary. There are many factors that affect international transfer pricing policies and make them more complicated than those used for domestic operations. These factors can be classified into two groups: (1) the interaction or conflict of pricing policies with other objectives (which are internal) of the firm, such as performance evaluation, motivation, and goal congruence; and (2) environmental variables that are external to the firm, such as foreign and domestic income taxes, tariffs, cash movement restrictions, foreign currency exchange risk, and conflict with foreign governments' policies.

If a MNE uses its transfer pricing policies for performance evaluation of its domestic and foreign subsidiaries and their managers, the MNE pricing method must be at market or competitive price, which is an essential factor under decentralization. The resulting net income or loss is the yardstick for the measurement of the subsidiary manager's ability to manage and control his area of responsibility (or his profit center). However, when the worldwide market for the transferred product is not competitive or there is no market for the intermediate product transferred, any transfer price other than the negotiated price will neither maintain autonomy or freedom in decision making nor motivate managers to adhere to the objectives of the company as a whole, which in turn will impair goal congruence.

Of environmental variables or external factors that affect MNEs in deciding on the appropriate transfer pricing policy to be used, one of the most important is the taxes to be paid to both foreign and U.S. governments as a result of transferring the goods across the borders of two different countries. The tax authorities in foreign countries and the Internal Revenue Service (IRS) of the United States are very much aware of the effect of the transfer price set by an MNE on taxes paid to each of the two tax authorities as a result of the existence of different tax structures of different countries. For example, a MNE can set a low transfer price for goods transferred from a subsidiary in country A with a high corporate tax to sell at cost to a subsidiary in country B where income taxes are lower. The result is that global tax liabilities of a MNE are less than before, and consequently the global profits will be higher. However, when the performance of each subsidiary is evaluated as a separate profit center, this transfer price will show lower profits for the subsidiary in country A and a higher profit for the subsidiary in country B. This will lead to conflicts between goals of the subsidiaries and those of the MNE.[8]

Another factor considered to be important when a MNE is setting up international transfer pricing policies is cash movement restrictions of foreign governments on moving cash outside the country. When a country is suffering from a problem of foreign exchange, the government may prohibit such movement or impose strong controls that limit the amount of cash, profit, or dividends that can be repatriated. This problem can be illustrated by assuming that country A, which is suffering from a lack of Japanese yen, imposes controls on all yen transactions. A seller subsidiary in country B, where there are yen or another currency convertible into yen, sells to a buyer subsidiary in country A, there are no restrictions on cash movements, at a higher price than the cost. The outcome of the transaction is to transfer the profits from country A to country B and then from country B to the home country.[9] Sidney Robbins and Robert Stobaugh concluded from their interviews with 39 U.S.-based MNEs that although tax minimization is usually a principal goal of transfer pricing, avoiding exchange controls is even more important.[10]

Import duties, tariffs, or customs can be high or low from one country to another and complicate the policies to establish the appropriate international transfer prices. If country B imposes import duties at the rate of 20% on the invoice (transfer) price, a subsidiary selling its goods from country A to another subsidiary in country B could reduce the import duties paid by lowering the transfer price below cost. However, governments may intervene, because country B's government may believe that lowering transfer prices is tax evasion, and at the same time, the customs authorities in country B believe that there are revenues forgone.

As can be seen from this discussion, the appropriate international transfer price used by a MNE and the one required to achieve certain objectives, such as performance evaluation and motivation, income tax minimization, avoidance of foreign exchange controls, or competitiveness, may or may not be the same. It is important to note that five criteria must be met for establishing an efficient international transfer pricing system:

1. The international transfer pricing policy should provide an adequate profit measurement to evaluate the performance of foreign subsidiaries and their managers in terms of their controllable divisional contributions to global profits.

2. It should provide adequate information to top management to be used as guidelines in managerial decision making.

3. It should increase the overall profit rate of the MNE; in other words, the MNE's overall performance must be improved by the use of the international transfer pricing system.

4. It should motivate foreign subsidiary managers to increase their efficiency and maximize their divisional profits in harmony with the objectives of top management.

5. It should minimize the international transaction costs for a MNE by minimizing border and income tax liabilities, foreign exchange risks, currency manipulation losses, and conflict with the foreign government's policies.

OUTLINE OF THIS BOOK

Chapter 2 discusses the process of designing and establishing a transfer pricing system for global operations of a MNE. It examines the requirements that should be satisfied to establish an efficient and effective system that will maximize the MNE's profits and minimize its international transaction costs, how the system can be used as an adequate profit yardstick to evaluate the foreign subsidiary managers' performance, and the profit-center concepts and their applications in the international environment.

In Chapter 3 the objectives of international transfer pricing systems are discussed, with more emphasis on reducing income taxes, minimizing tariffs, strengthening competitive position in international markets, and many other objectives. Chapter 4 is concerned with the techniques of international transfer pricing. It includes actual unit variable costs, actual unit costs, budgeted or standard unit variable/total costs, the cost-plus method, the market price method, and other techniques.

Chapter 5 covers the use of international transfer pricing policies as input for mangement's decision-making process. It discusses what types of decisions are made for international operations, and how MNEs should design the appropriate international transfer pricing system that can help them in making optimum capital budgeting decisions by choosing the best alternative that will achieve their global objectives in the long run.

Chapter 6 examines the relationship between international transfer pricing and taxation. It discusses the significant effect of different tax systems and tax rates of different countries on transfer pricing decisions and consequently on the production costs and revenues of MNEs. It also examines Section 482 of the Internal Revenue Code and its effect on MNE's top-management decisions in terms of how to avoid double taxation and minimize tax liabilities.

Chapter 7 covers environmental factors and their effect on international transfer pricing policies and the decision-making process in utilizing and allocating economic, financial, and human resources. The results, summary, and conclusions of this study are the subject of Chapter 8.

Appendix A includes Section 482 of the U.S. Internal Revenue Code allocation of income and deductions among taxpayers. Appendix B includes management accounting guidelines on Internal Transfer pricing used by the Institute of Cost and Management Accountants (ICMA, London).

NOTES

1. American Accounting Association, "Report of the Committee on International Accounting," *Accounting Review* 48 (1973 Supplement): 122–33.

2. D. T. Otley and A. J. Berry, "Control, Organization, and Accounting," in *Reading in Cost Accounting, Budgeting, and Control*, ed. William E. Thomas, 6th ed., (Cincinnati: South Western Publishing Co., 1983), 15.

3. Stefan H. Robock and Kenneth Simmonds, *International Business and Multinational Enterprises*, 3rd ed. (Homewood, Ill.: Richard D. Irwin, 1983), 392–93.

4. R. Hal Mason, Robert R. Miller, and Dale R. Weigel, *International Business*, 2nd ed. (New York: John Wiley and Sons, 1981), 346.

5. Donald A. Ball and Wendell H. McCulloch, Jr., *International Business*, 2nd ed. (Plano, Tex.: Business Publications, 1985), 443–44.

6. For more details see David Solomons, *Divisional Performance: Measurement and Control*, (Homewood, Ill.: Richard D. Irwin, 1965) 81–84; Ralph L. Benke, Jr., and James Don Edwards, *Transfer Pricing Techniques and Uses* (New York: National Association of Accountants, 1980), 75–80.

7. American Accounting Association, "Report of the Committee" (1973): 152.

8. Frederick D. S. Choi and Gerhard G. Mueller, *International Accounting* (Englewood Cliffs, N.J.: Prentice-Hall, 1984), 435.

9. Ball and McCulloch, *International Business*, 446.

10. Sidney M. Robbins and Robert B. Stobaugh, *Money in the Multinational Enterprise* (New York: Basic Books, 1973), 92.

2

Establishing International Transfer Pricing Systems

A transfer price is set and used by MNEs to quantify the goods transferred from one subsidiary domiciled in a specific country to a subsidiary located in another country. The dynamic growth of most MNEs by going abroad and exploring more and more business opportunities in other countries necessitated more delegation of authority and responsibility with more autonomy for foreign subsidiary managers, which opened the door for more decentralization and intracompany pricing problems.

Since the transfer price for a product has an important effect on performance evaluation of individual foreign subsidiary managers, their motivation, divisional profitability, and the global profits as well, top management should devote special attention to designing international transfer pricing policies. A soundly developed policy could lead to better goal congruence, better performance evaluation measures, lower taxes and tariffs, more motivated managers, fewer exchange risks, and better competitive positions in foreign countries and international markets.

In designing international transfer pricing systems, four major components should be considered: (*a*) inputs, (*b*) process, (*c*) objectives, and (*d*) output. The relationship among the four components of the system is illustrated in Figure 2.1. Inputs and process will be discussed in this chapter, while objectives will be examined in Chapter 3. The output of a well-designed international transfer pricing system will be an appropriate international transfer price that will be the optimum one to achieve all of management's objectives.

Figure 2.1
The Relationship among the Components of the International
Transfer Pricing System

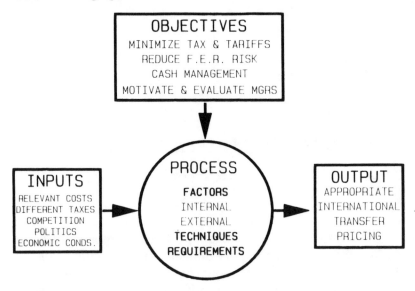

THE INPUTS OF AN INTERNATIONAL TRANSFER PRICING SYSTEM

The inputs of an international transfer pricing system (ITP) consist of six factors to be considered in deciding the appropriate price to be charged for goods transferred across the border from one country to another. These inputs are (1) relevant cost information, (2) differential income tax rates, (3) exchange risks, (4) restrictions on cash transfers, (5) import/export tariffs, and (6) competition in foreign markets.

In this chapter the effect of each input variable will be considered as if all other variables are held constant. In a later chapter the effect of all input variables will be considered in a real-world model for the established appropriate international transfer pricing system. The relationship between the input factors and the international transfer pricing system is illustrated in Figure 2.2.

Relevant Cost Information

ITP policies need information about costs and revenues of all goods and services transferred to use it for coordination and integration

Figure 2.2
The Input Factors of the International Transfer Pricing System

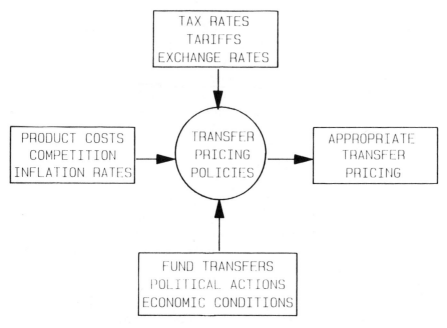

purposes. Cost information is a major input for ITP systems, because this is one of the most important factors in making decisions on transfer pricing. The question is: What cost information is relevant to the manager's decision on pricing of goods transferred out of his division or subsidiary?

Relevant costs are defined as those expected future costs that will make the difference between charging a higher or lower price for goods transferred among subsidiaries of the same MNE in different countries. A foreign subsidiary manager must have the relevant cost information, the ability to use it in the decision-making process, and the understanding of its effect on both his divisional profitability and the global profits of his firm.

A cost objective is the product whose cost is to be determined. Cost objective includes direct materials, direct labor, and manufacturing overhead. Other costs include selling and administrative expenses that are related to a foreign subsidiary plus other costs allocated by the headquarters of the MNE. These costs are classified into variable and fixed. Variable costs vary directly and proportionately with the activity level, while fixed costs do not change with the activity level. Variable costs include such items as direct raw materials, direct labor, sales commissions, and transportation costs. Fixed costs include such items as factory rent, salaries for supervisors, and depreciation of factory equipment.

Some costs cannot be described by a single cost behavior pattern because they are partially variable and partially fixed. Many techniques have been developed for identifying the variable and fixed portions, including industrial engineering, account analysis, visual fit, high-low, and regression analysis.

In designing an ITP system, managers must decide which inventory-costing alternative to choose. This decision will have an effect on net income of both the foreign subsidiary unit and the global enterprise, on the evaluation of foreign subsidiary managers' performance, and on international transfer pricing decisions.[1]

There are two inventory-costing methods used in practice: absorption and variable costing. Absorption (or full) costing includes direct materials, direct labor, and both variable and fixed factory overhead as the cost of a product; that is, product costs include both direct and indirect manufacturing costs. Under this method, fixed manufacturing costs are absorbed by the product transferred and are part of the costs of goods sold or transferred and ending inventories.

Variable (or direct) costing includes only variable manufacturing costs as the cost of a product; that is, product costs include direct materials, direct labor, and variable manufacturing costs. All fixed manufacturing costs are excluded from the inventoriable costs and are expensed during the fiscal year in which they are incurred together with all selling and administrative expenses.

As an example, let us assume that a subsidiary in country A produces 20,000 units of its product. Fixed manufacturing costs were $15,000, variable manufacturing costs were $3.50 per unit ($2 for direct material, $1 for direct labor, and 50 cents for variable factory overhead), variable selling costs were 30 cents per unit sold, and fixed selling and administrative expenses were $5,500. Sales for 1986 were 16,000 units (including 6,000 transferred to other foreign subsidiaries) at $5 per unit. The net income of the foreign subsidiary for the year under both absorption and direct costing methods can be seen in Table 2.1.

The difference in net income for the foreign subsidiary in year 1986 between the two costing methods is caused entirely by the fixed factory

Table 2.1
Absorption and Variable Costing for a Foreign Subsidiary

Absorption Costing

```
Sales 16,000 at $5                                          80,000
Less:
   Cost of goods sold & transferred
   Beg. inventory                               -0-
         Direct materials    20,000 x $2 = 40,000
         Direct labor        20,000 x $1 = 20,000
         Factory overhead
         Variable 20,000 x .50 = 10,000
         Fixed    20,000 x .75 = 15,000      25,000
   Cost of goods available for sale           85,000
 --Ending inventories (20,000-16,000)
                  4,000 x $4.25 =             17,000
   Cost of goods sold                                       68,000
The foreign subsidiary gross profit                        12,000
Less: selling & administrative expenses
         Variable .30 x 16,000 =               4,800
         Fixed                  =              5,500
                                                            10,300
The foreign subsidiary net income                           1,700
```
===

Variable (Direct) Costing

```
Sales 16,000 at $5                                          80,000
Less Total variable costs
   Manufacturing
         Direct materials
            20,000 x $2          =            40,000
         Direct labor
            20,000 x $1          =            20,000
         Factory overhead (variable only)
            20,000 x 50 cents    =            10,000
         Variable mfg. cost of goods          70,000
            available for sale or transfer
Less: Ending inventory
            4,000 x 3.50         =           (14,000)
         Variable cost of goods sold          56,000
            and transferred
         + Variable selling & adm exp.
            .30 x 16,000         =             4,800
Total variable manufacturing costs                         60,800
Total foreign subsidiary contributions margin              19,200

Less: Total fixed costs
         Manufacturing                        15,000
         Selling and administrative            5,500       (20,500)
The foreign subsidiary net loss                           ( 1,300)
```

=========

overhead of $3,000 (4,000 units at 75 cents per unit). This $3,000 is absorbed by the unsold products and included in the ending inventory when absorption costing is used and expensed only when the products are sold or transferred out. Therefore, the ending inventory included current fixed factory overhead costs of $3,000 that are not expensed until a future year. Under the variable costing method, fixed factory overhead is not inventoried. The $3,000 is included in the net income of 1987, and the net income of $1,700 under absorption costing is switched to a net loss of $1,300 under variable costing for the foreign subsidiary. The absorption costing method is the generally accepted method of product costing for external reporting, and the variable costing method is used to prepare internal financial reports to assist in making economic decisions.

Does it make any difference which method the firm should choose? Realistically, it depends on what transfer pricing technique the MNE is using or intends to use, assuming that the transfer pricing decision is made at the parent's level. If the intention is to use unit variable actual (or standard) cost or unit variable cost plus a markup, the variable costing method is more appropriate. However, with the use of the unit full cost (actual or standard) or unit full cost-plus, the absorption costing method is preferable.

Differential Income Tax Rates

The income tax policies and regulations of governments of different countries are not the same or even close to each other. International taxation has a significant effect on MNEs in making their management decisions. "Taxation affects where a MNE invests, how it markets its products, what form of business organization it selects, when and where to remit cash, how to finance—and of course—the choice of a transfer price."[2] If tax rates of different countries were the same, there would be no reason to prefer a higher transfer price over a lower one for the global profits of a MNE.

Both the host and home governments are interested in profits realized by a MNE, and transfer prices make a big difference in the amounts of income taxes paid to either government. Tax authorities of both countries have become very much aware of the significant impact of the differences in the two tax structures on MNEs in deciding at what price to transfer goods or services from one country to another. From a MNE's point of view, the transfer of goods and services from one subsidiary to another in a different country generates taxable revenues and tax-deductible costs in different countries. Section 482 of the U.S. Internal Revenue Code (see Appendix A) gives the Internal Revenue Service agent the authority to reallocate gross income, deductions, credits, or allowances in intracorporate transactions in order to prevent tax evasion or to reflect more clearly a fair allocation of income.

Exchange Risk

Foreign exchange risk is defined as "the risk of a change (gain or loss) in the company's future economic value resulting from a change in exchange rates."[3] For MNEs, the exchange risk is connected with the firm's cash flows in different currencies, and any change in exchange rates between two different currencies has a direct effect on the value in the base currency of funds to be converted from one foreign currency to another.[4] Devaluation of the currency of the home country pushes the foreign sale of goods up and the home-country sales down. This directly affects MNEs because it increases the foreign currencies they are holding.

Since MNEs' activities involve many countries, they must deal with many currencies. The value of a currency frequently changes by either devaluation or appreciation. Foreign exchange risk affects both companies with international operations and those with receivables and payables to be collected or paid in foreign currencies.[5]

Restrictions on Cash Transfers

Host governments, especially of third world countries, devise different policies such as profit repatriations and/or tax exchange controls, to regulate MNEs' activities for the purpose of protecting their own local industries. MNEs set international transfer pricing policies as a way to overcome these restrictions.[6] Sidney Robbins and Robert Stobaugh in their interviews with 39 U.S.-based MNEs concluded that although income tax minimization is a major objective of using transfer pricing, avoiding exchange controls is even more important.[7]

Exchange controls with profit repatriation restrictions have been ranked as one of the most important factors in setting international transfer prices by MNEs. Most developing countries have been using exchange control restrictions to avoid outflows of foreign funds outside the country.[8] However, MNEs use their international transfer pricing policies to overcome these restrictions imposed by host governments and to decide how much cash will be sent out of the host countries or to the home country as part of their profits.

Tariffs

The words tariffs, customs, and import duties are used interchangeably. Transfer pricing policies can be used to reduce tariffs imposed on imports into the country or exports outside the country. Low transfer prices for imports reduce the payments of high tariffs.

In less developed countries the use of low transfer pricing on imports may significantly affect the balance of payments of those countries, especially when they import huge quantities from the same MNEs. On the other hand, MNEs may impose a higher transfer price for goods transferred to subsidiaries of foreign countries with low duty rates.

However, combining both tariffs and income taxes together complicates the decison of setting up the appropriate transfer prices, as will be discussed in Chapter 3, especially in countries where there are low duties with high income tax rates. In addition, export duties of the country where the foreign subsidiary (the seller) is located should be considered along with the import duties of the country where the buying subsidiary is located, which, in turn, will never coincide with the transfer pricing strategies of MNEs.

The trade-off between tariffs and income taxes is more difficult than it looks. A MNE cannot charge two different subsidiaries of the same country two different transfer prices for the same goods. Host governments have started to look more closely at the transfer pricing policies of MNEs investing in their countries until they make sure that the tax revenues of the country, and consequently the balance of payments, are not significantly affected.

Competition

When a new foreign subsidiary is starting a new business overseas, competition is another factor that should be considered in establishing international transfer pricing policies. A MNE can set a low transfer price for goods shipped to the new foreign subsidiary to strengthen its financial and competitive position in the first years of business. However, this may open the door for the intervention of host governments to protect their local industries if the selling prices of the new subsidiary are much lower than those of other domestic industries of the host country. A MNE can charge high international transfer prices for imported goods to report lower profits on its foreign subsidiaries to avoid host governments' interference when they show higher profitability, or charge low transfer prices to discourage any new firms from entering the market to compete with them.

International transfer pricing policies have become the most controversial issue in MNEs in reporting the results of their international business transactions. The top management of an MNE tries to accomplish the following:

1. to minimize foreign exchange losses

2. to avoid exchange control restrictions on cash outflows

3. to pay lower tariffs on both imports and exports

4. to minimize total income tax liability to be paid for both home- and host-country governments by charging low international transfer prices for goods and services transferred into countries with low income tax rates for the buying subsidiaries and charging high prices for goods and services transferred into countries with high income tax rates

5. to help foreign subsidiaries to compete with other firms in foreign countries, to achieve goal congruence between foreign subsidiary objectives and overall MNE objectives, to provide subsidiary managers with relevant information for decision making, to evaluate the performance of foreign subsidiaries and their managers on an objective basis, and to allocate their financial, economic, and human resources efficiently.

A MNE, when trying to establish its international transfer pricing policies, may find a great degree of conflict among all these factors. Countries with low income tax rates may impose higher tariffs on goods transferred into the country. Countries with serious problems with foreign exchange may use restrictive monetary policies to completely prohibit or place restraints on cash movements that can be repatriated. Moreover, there is conflict between charging low international transfer prices to help foreign subsidiaries, newly established, to compete or survive in a country by showing artificially higher profits and then using these profits for performance evaluation of foreign subsidiary managers.

THE PROCESS OF ESTABLISHING INTERNATIONAL TRANSFER PRICING SYSTEMS

A process can be a series of actions, changes, or functions that bring about a particular result. The process of an international transfer pricing system includes a series of factors affecting the decision to choose the appropriate international transfer pricing technique that should meet specific requirements to achieve the MNE's objectives.

In discussing the process of the ITP systems, there are four elements to be included: (1) the factors affecting the decision, (2) different techniques to choose from, (3) specific requirements to be met, and (4) the objectives of ITP systems. Items 1 and 3 are discussed in detail in this chapter, and items 2 and 4 will be discussed later in two separate chapters.

Factors Affecting International Transfer Pricing Systems

There are many factors that have a significant effect on designing an appropriate international transfer pricing system. These factors can be classified into internal factors and external factors. In designing international transfer pricing policies, all internal as well as external factors should be considered. Otherwise, many problems such as suboptimal decisions, disruption in the operating process, and negative behavioral actions may be the result.

Internal factors are behavioral, organizational, managerial, and motivational issues. Degree of decentralization, interdependence, management control system, goal congruence, motivation, and performance evaluation are just a few examples. These and other related issues that have an effect on establishing a well-designed international transfer pricing system are discussed here.

First, the degree of decentralization or centralization of managerial decision making for transfer pricing is an important issue. Complete decentralization that includes the delegation of authority for decision making of production and sales is used only when foreign subsidiaries buy and sell on the market. Foreign or domestic subsidiary managers are assumed to have freedom in making decisions for production and sales, thus making their decisions more quickly, relieving top management of making operating decisions, and being evaluated on the basis of operational measurement performance.

However, decentralization has its own drawbacks or side effects on a MNE. The biggest problem is "dysfunctional decision making," which may lead to conflict between subsidiary and corporate objectives. Another problem is that relevant information for making decisions is gathered at the subsidiary level for transfer pricing rather than in the home country; however, because of independence of each foreign or domestic subsidiary from another, the relevant information is not fully communicated among subsidiary managers.[9]

Second, the degree of interdependence among foreign and domestic subsidiaries affects the establishing of a well-designed ITP system. If the decisions or actions of one subsidiary affect the business of one or more of the others in other countries, a high degree of interdependence of international operations exists. With highly interrelated international operations, subsidiary managers may make their decisions without considering the effects on other subsidiaries of the same MNE. As a result, these managerial decisions may optimize the individual manager's profits at the expense of others, which in turn will not lead to optimal global profits.

Third, the profit-center concept has been used by many MNEs as the main basis of domestic performance evaluation. A subsidiary manager under this concept makes the major decisions relating to profit-center costs and revenues. Since he is able to influence the results of operations, he is accountable for and evaluated on the basis of these results, which are the profits of the profit centers.

A profit center is usually characterized by independence, autonomy, and freedom in decision making. A subsidiary manager should try to achieve the highest possible profits for his subsidiary by buying from other subsidiaries of the same MNE or from the market at the lowest price and selling to others at the highest price. These managers are actually using the international transfer prices that maximize their profits and consequently show better performance for their subsidiaries. However, the profit-center concept in a MNE may not work well for the following reasons:

1. Transfer pricing policies are usually set in MNEs to facilitate cash movements where currency restrictions exist and to minimize taxes. Therefore, transfer pricing policies are not complementary to the profit-center concept. Consequently, performance evaluation cannot be achieved properly using the traditional management techniques.

2. With the existence of different inflation rates and other sociological, economic, legal, political, and educational conditions among countries, top management may have trouble understanding each country's situation and so be less able to evaluate what is good or bad profit performance abroad. Profit centers are likely, therefore, to have more utility for domestic than foreign subsidiaries.[10]

3. Domestic company activities are often organized by independent profit or investment centers. Under these decentralized systems, subsidiary managers are given the authority to make decisions directly affecting their activities. Under these conditions, rate of return on investment (ROI) as a measure of performance is acceptable. However, such evaluation systems may not function well for MNEs because foreign operations are often established for strategic economic reasons rather than for profit maximization; thus many of these operations cannot be measured precisely or quantitatively by ROI.[11]

4. Many times the units of a MNE are integrated and managed as a coordinated whole, which means that the major decisions affecting profits are made centrally for all units. Therefore, the profit-center concept may be irrelevant.[12]

If there is no high degree of independence, and the foreign subsidiary has no control over the transfer price, then the pseudo–profit-center concept is used. A pseudo–profit center is "a responsibility center in which profit is based on internal sales or purchases at artificial prices."[13] Foreign subsidiary managers of the pseudo–profit center use artificial profits and have control only over costs, and it is more likely to be considered as a cost center. In this case, international transfer prices are only used for performance evaluation purposes.[14]

Fourth, the management control process (MCP) is another factor affecting ITP systems. There are two major objectives of the process: (1) to guide subsidiary managers to achieve the MNE's objectives, and (2) to measure the results of the subsidiary's performance against the MNE's objectives. It is essential for a MNE to operate and manage its international operations within the objectives of its management control process and make sure that the objectives of both management control process and ITP are consistent.[15]

The main purpose in designing the MCP is to achieve goal congruence, which is the equality of the sum of individual goals with those of the MNE. The international transfer price should help both the buying and selling subsidiaries to make the right decisions to maximize their own profits and at the same time the global profits of the MNE as a whole. However, it is more likely that transfer prices may create conflicts between the buying and selling subsidiaries because the buying subsidiary tries to use the lowest possible transfer price to maximize its profits while the selling subsidiary tries to sell at the highest possible price.

Fifth, the use of ITP systems may motivate subsidiary managers to work in their own divisional self-interest because they are motivated by the "presumed behavioral advantage" of operating with a high degree of autonomy.[16] At the same time, organizational objectives should be achieved by being motivated to work for the best interest of the MNE as a whole. However, subsidiary managers may choose transfer pricing methods that are not compatible with the MNE's long-term objectives.[17]

Finally, performance evaluation of the subsidiaries and their managers is among the important factors affecting international transfer pricing policies. Transfer pricing techniques should not be used by subsidiary managers to manipulate their costs or profits for the purpose of creating "the illusion of better or worse performance" than has actually happened.[18]

Performance evaluation reports based on a transfer price set by top management do not reflect how much the foreign or domestic subsidiary or its manager contributes to the global profits unless the international transfer price among subsidiaries is identical to the market price of the intermediate product. Under these circumstances, the contribution of the subsidiary, measured by the market price, will be important for managers and central management, who use this information for the evaluation of the subsidiary's profitability and make decisions either to continue or discontinue their investments in this subsidiary.[19]

However, when there is no market for the intermediate products transferred internally among the subsidiaries, conflict is likely to arise in MNEs between subsidiary managers because of the opposing interests of the buyer subsidiary, which wants to be charged with the lowest possible transfer price, and the selling subsidiary, which wants to achieve the highest possible divisional profits by charging the highest possible transfer price.

The problem is more complicated when we look at all factors affecting transfer pricing policies combined together. Different income tax rates of different countries, different tariffs, and different cash flow restrictions, on the one hand, and motivation, performance evaluation, goal congruence, and profit center or pseudo-profit centers, on the other hand, require different transfer prices for the same goods transferred across the border. It is obvious that international transfer prices as used now in practice, at which goods are traded internally among different subsidiaries of different countries of MNEs, can significantly distort the profitability of foreign subsidiaries and their managers.

In addition to internal factors, there are external factors that can have an effect on the decision of what transfer price should be charged: (a) market conditions in foreign countries, (b) economic conditions, and (c) currency appreciation or devaluation. Foreign government intervention puts many restrictions on MNEs as they do business there. There are many ways for governments to intervene in the business of MNEs. They may increase or decrease prices of imports and exports through tariffs, quotas, and taxes, or they may intervene in foreign exchange rates. They also may restrict the amount of profits a MNE can transfer to reduce pressure on the balance of payments of the host country. All of these factors have significant effects on MNEs in setting the appropriate transfer prices. Transfer prices are also affected by the competitive position of subsidiaries in foreign countries. This position may need to be strengthened by charging low transfer prices for the input or high prices for the output, or to be weakened to avoid any potential government intervention.

Requirements for International Transfer Pricing Policies

An international transfer pricing policy should meet specific requirements if a MNE wants to achieve its objectives. Any transfer pricing method should provide an adequate measurement of the performance of both foreign subsidiaries and their managers. It should measure the manager's controllable contribution toward the global profit in an objective and operational way that must be consistent with the global objectives of the MNE and, at the same time, motivate managers toward instituting better performance.

It should provide top management with relevant information to decide to expand, continue, or discontinue its operations in specific locations of foreign countries. International intracompany pricing information plays a major role as an input for the decision-making process and in presenting a realistic profit picture of subsidiary performance.

The ITP policy should minimize income tax liability and tariffs (import/export duties) that MNEs pay for both host and home governments. In this case, the appropriate international transfer price should come up with the lowest possible total tax liability of MNEs to be paid, including both income taxes and tariffs combined.

Finally, it should reduce or alleviate the conflict between the MNE's objectives and foreign governments' objectives. MNEs should understand the needs of foreign governments and try to utilize the total economic and human resources in the best interests of both their own and foreign governments to avoid any possibility of profit repatriation, restrictions on cash movements or exchange control, expropriations, or any possible limitations imposed on MNEs' international activities that have a significant negative effect on global profits over the long run.

SUMMARY

Four major characteristics of ITP systems are identified in this chapter: (a) input, (b) process, (c) objectives, and (d) output. The inputs of an ITP system consist of seven factors to be considered in deciding the appropriate price to be charged for goods transferred through the border from one country to another. These inputs are (1) relevant cost information, (2) differential income tax rates, (3) foreign exchange risks, (4) restriction on cash transfers, (5) tariffs, and (6) competition.

The process of an ITP system includes a series of factors affecting the decision to choose an appropriate ITP technique, which should meet specific requirements to achieve the MNE's objectives. In discussing the process of an ITP system, four elements should be considered: (1) the factors affecting the decision, (2) different techniques to choose from, (3) specific requirements to be met, and (4) the objectives of ITP systems. Items 1 and 3 were analyzed and discussed in detail in this chapter; items 2 and 4 will be discussed in the following two chapters.

NOTES

1. Charles T. Horngren and George Foster, *Cost Accounting: A Managerial Emphasis*, 6th ed. (Englewood Cliffs, N.J.: Prentice-Hall, 1987) 252.

2. Gerhard G. Mueller, Helen Gernon, and Gary Meek, *Accounting: An International Perspective* (Homewood, Ill.: Richard D. Irwin, 1987), 146.

3. Lars Oxelheim, *International Financial Market Fluctuations* (New York: John Wiley and Sons, 1985), 61.

4. Ibid.

5. Stefan H. Robock and Kenneth Simmonds, *International Business and Multinational Enterprises*, 3rd ed. (Homewood, Ill.: Richard D. Irwin, 1983), 536.

6. H. Seung Kim and Stephen W. Miller, "Constituents of the International Transfer Pricing Decisions," *Columbia Journal of World Business* (Spring 1979): 72.

7. Sidney M. Robbins and Robert B. Stobaugh, *Money in the Multinational Enterprise* (New York: Basic Books, 1973), 72.

8. Kim and Miller, "Constituents," 72.

9. Lynette L. Knowles and Ike Mathur, "Factors Influencing the Designing of International Transfer Pricing Systems," *Management Finance* 11 (1985): 18.

10. George M. Scott, "Planning, Control, and Performance Evaluation Systems in International Operations," *Cost and Management* (Canada) (January–February 1977): 8.

11. Frederick D. S. Choi, "Global Finance and Accounting Uniformity," *University of Michigan Business Review* (September 1976): 48.

12. Scott, "Planning," 8–9.

13. Ralph L. Benke, Jr., and James Don Edwards, "Should You Use Transfer Pricing to Create Pseudo-Profit Centers?" *Management Accounting* (February 1981): 36.

14. Ralph L. Benke, Jr., and James Don Edwards, *Transfer Pricing Techniques and Uses* (New York: National Association of Accountants, 1980), 25.

15. Knowles and Mathur, "Factors Influencing the Designing of International Transfer Pricing Systems," 17.

16. See A. Rashad Abdel-Khalik and Edward J. Lusk, "Transfer Pricing: A Synthesis," *Accounting Review* 69 (January 1974): 8.

17. Knowles and Mathur, "Factors Influencing the Designing of International Transfer Pricing Systems," 17.

18. Benke and Edwards, *Transfer Pricing Techniques and Uses* 21.

19. Joshua Ronen and George McKinney, "Transfer Pricing for Divisional Autonomy," *Journal of Accounting Research* 8 (Spring 1970): 100.

3

Objectives of International Transfer Pricing Systems

Theoretically, MNEs have the ability to use their international transfer pricing policies to maximize their global profits. Practically, developing these policies is the most difficult pricing problem, one more complicated than developing domestic transfer pricing policies. A MNE has to manage its production and marketing policies in a world characterized by different international tax rates, foreign exchange rates, governmental regulations, currency manipulation, and other economic and social problems. Such market characteristics create high transaction costs for a MNE when it uses its regular marketing policies. It is important for MNEs to create an internal market if they want to avoid these problems and any costs associated with them.[1] Allocation of resources among domestic and foreign subsidiaries requires the central management of a MNE to set up the appropriate transfer price to achieve certain objectives.

Central top management in the home country and both domestic and foreign subsidiary managers must understand the objectives for using transfer pricing policies within their organizations. Top management and managers need to know how these usually interrelated objectives can affect each other.[2]

An international transfer pricing (ITP) system should achieve two different groups of objectives. The first group includes (1) consistency with the system of performance evaluation; (2) motivation of subsidiary managers; and (3) achievement of goal congruence. The second group consists of certain objectives that are more relevant to the international operations. These objectives include (1) reduction of income taxes, (2) reduction of tariffs on imports and exports, (3) minimization of foreign exchange risks, (4) avoidance of a conflict with host countries' governments, (5) management of cash flow, and (6) competitiveness in the international markets.

However, any manipulation of transfer pricing policies by MNEs may have a significant impact on many areas of the worldwide economy, including both home and host countries. The impact of transfer pricing policies includes effects on balance of payments and foreign and domestic formation of capital investment. By charging higher transfer prices on goods transferred into the country to a subsidiary, the MNE can limit a subsidiary's export abilities or avoid controls on foreign remittance by "tapping-off excess profits."[3] Imposing low transfer pricing on sales of foreign subsidiaries will reduce customs duty payments and help subsidiaries to compete in foreign markets against other local competitors.[4]

The purpose of this chapter is to identify, at the international level, different objectives of estabishing transfer pricing systems, to investigate how MNEs can achieve all, most, or few of these objectives, and to point out significant problems MNEs might face when they try to achieve these objectives. The second group of objectives will be discussed first because of their significant impact on international operations.

REDUCTION OF INCOME TAXES

One of the most important objectives of an international transfer pricing system is believed to be reducing the global income tax liability of a MNE. Tax reduction can be achieved by transferring goods to countries with low income tax rates at the lowest possible transfer prices and by transferring goods out of these countries at the highest possible transfer prices. In countries with high income tax rates, goods transferred into the country should be at the highest possible transfer prices, and goods transferred out of them should be at the lowest possible prices.

International transfer pricing policies are generally set to maximize the after-tax profitability of worldwide business transactions. The minimization of income tax liabilities for a MNE has been considered as the most significant factor or objective in designing ITP policies, and consequently, if a transfer price shifts profits from a country with high tax rates to a country with low tax rates, the global profits will be maximized.[5]

To illustrate the income tax effects on setting international transfer prices, let us assume that foreign subsidiary A produces 20,000 units and sells 16,000 units to subsidiary B at $5.00 a unit. B in turn sells these units for $12.00 a unit to an unrelated customer.

As can be seen from Table 3.1, the income tax rate of country A is 30% and that of country B is 50%. As a result of using different transfer prices, there is a significant change in the net income of both foreign subsidiaries and the consolidated net income of the MNE as a whole. With the low transfer price, subsidiary A sells at $5.00 per unit and pays income taxes of $510, subsidiary B pays income tax liability of $18,500, and the MNE pays a total tax liability of $19,010 and realizes a consolidated net income of $19,690. Under the high transfer price policy, A's income taxes go up to $10,110 while B's taxes go down to $2,500, the combined tax liabilities go from $19,010 down to $12,610, and the consolidated net income goes from $19,690 up to $26,090. The consequences of charging a higher transfer price are (1) a decrease in total tax liabilities by $6,400 ($19,010 − $12,610) and (2) an increase in the consolidated net income by the same amount.

The general rule for the strategy of MNEs, if the sole corporate objective is to minimize total tax liability, should be to transfer most of the profits to the foreign subsidiaries in the tax-haven countries, as can be seen in Figure 3.1. However, the manipulation of international transfer pricing policies only for reducing income taxes has caused the governmental tax authorities, including the U.S. Internal Revenue Service (IRS), to intervene to ensure that there is no tax evasion and the country does not lose its tax revenue under the transfer pricing shield. Moreover, there are many factors besides income tax minimization that should be considered by MNEs in designing their ITP systems, such as motivation and performance evaluation of foreign subsidiary managers, competitiveness in foreign markets, and foreign exchange risks.

A survey by H. Seung Kim and Stephen W. Miller indicated that in the past, MNEs considered reducing income taxes as the most important objective in designing their ITP systems. Now, tax reduction is only a minor factor among many others, and the company's overall objective rather than income tax liability should be a major concern.[6]

Along with the reduction of global income tax liability, a major problem is how to coordinate the tax effect of transferred goods

Table 3.1
The Tax Effect of High versus Low International Transfer Pricing

	A	B	THE GLOBE
LOW TRANSFER PRICE			
SALES			
16,000 @ $5.00	$80,000		
16,000 @ $12.00		$192,000	$192,000
LESS: COST OF G.S.	(68,000)	(80,000)	(68,000)
GROSS PROFIT	12,000	112,000	124,000
LESS: S, A, & G EXP.	(10,300)	(75,000)	(85,300)
NET INCOME BEFORE TAX	1,700	37,000	38,700
LESS: INCOME TAX			
(30% AND 50%)	(510)	(18,500)	(19,010)
NET INCOME	1,190	18,500	19,690
HIGH TRANSFER PRICE			
SALES			
16,000 @ $7.00	$112,000		
16,000 @ $12.00		$192,000	$192,000
LESS: COST OF G. S.	(68,000)	(112,000)	(68,000)
GROSS PROFIT	44,000	80,000	124,000
LESS: S, A, & G EXP.	(10,300)	(75,000)	(85,300)
NET INCOME BEFORE TAX	33,700	5,000	38,700
LESS: INCOME TAX			
(30% AND 50%)	(10,110)	(2,500)	(12,610)
NET INCOME	23,590	2,500	26,090

among different countries to come up with the optimal transfer price. To set the appropriate transfer price for tax reduction, it is very important to determine the tax effects of (1) different ways of taxing imports and exports by imposing duties and customs on them, and (2) different tax rate structures and the methods of taxing MNEs' profits used by host countries.

It is not an easy task to determine the results of these effects on MNEs' global profits because they are frequently and rapidly changed by host- and home-country governments to achieve some economic, political, or social objectives for their own countries. In the United States the IRS is concerned that MNEs may reduce their tax liabilities by using transfer prices to shift profits from multinational local

Figure 3.1
Transfer Pricing Strategies under Different Tax Rates of
Different Countries

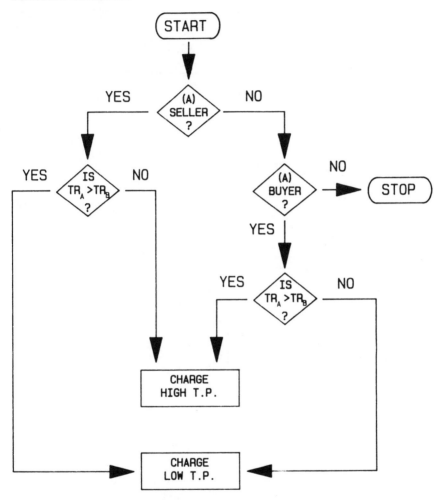

businesses to businesses in countries with low tax rates. Section 482 of the Internal Revenue Code gives the IRS the power to reallocate income and deductions among subsidiaries of a MNE if it finds that this is necessary to prevent any illegal reduction of taxes (that is, tax evasion). Under this section, all transfer prices should generally be established according to arm's-length market values on any transactions between affiliates.

MNEs, under Section 482 (see Appendix A), are not allowed to use any transfer price that will maximize their global profits other than an arms-length price or any pricing method other than the following, which are considered arm's-length: (1) the comparable uncontrolled price method; (2) the resale price method; and (3) the cost-plus method. However, if the ITP policies of a MNE were designed only to comply with Section 482 of the Internal Revenue Code, there would not be effective systems to measure managers' performance, motivate them to control the costs of their subsidiaries, or maximize the global profits of the MNE as a whole.

REDUCTION OF TARIFFS

Tariffs are the most widely used trade restrictions by foreign countries and can be imposed on either imports or exports. Tariffs on imports are used as a way of reducing the volume of imports coming into the country and to protect local industries. MNEs use transfer pricing policies as a way to reduce import or export tariffs and to avoid paying high tariffs to governments, and consequently to reduce their global costs and maximize their global profits. However, the use of transfer pricing for both reduction of income taxes and tariffs at the same time complicates the transfer pricing system.

As an example, let us assume that the foreign subsidiary in country B must pay tariffs at the rate of 15%, and that the income tax rates of countries A and B are 30% and 50% respectively. Then increasing the transfer price will increase the tariffs that subsidiary B must pay, assuming that the tariffs are imposed on the invoice transfer price. The combined effect of tax and tariff with the increased transfer price is shown in Table 3.2.

Under the low transfer price policy of $5.00 per unit, import tariffs of $12,000 (15% of $80,000) are paid to the government of country B, while the income tax paid will decline by a $6,000 tax shield (50% of $12,000) since import tariffs are assumed to be tax-deductible in country B. Total income taxes and import tariffs to be paid are $25,010. Under the high transfer price policy, the import tariffs increase from $12,000 to $14,400 (a difference of $2,400), while at the same time B's income taxes are lowered by $9,200. Total taxes and tariffs decrease by $2,000 from $25,010 to $23,010. The high transfer price policy is still preferable because of the $2,000 increase in global profits.

Table 3.2
The Effect of Transfer Pricing, Income Taxes, and Tariffs
on Net Income

	A	B	THE GLOBE
LOW TRANSFER PRICE:			
SALES			
16,000 @ $5.00	$80,000		
16,000 @ $12.00		$192,000	$192,000
LESS: COST OF G. S.	(68,000)	(80,000)	(68,000)
IMPORT CUSTOMS			
@ 15%		(12,000)	(12,000)
GROSS PROFIT	12,000	100,000	112,000
LESS: S, A, & G EXP.	(10,300)	(75,000)	(85,300)
NET INCOME BEFORE TAX	1,700	25,000	26,700
LESS: INCOME TAX			
(30% & 50%)	(510)	(12,500)	(13,010)
NET INCOME	1,190	12,500	13,690
HIGH TRANSFER PRICE:			
SALES			
16,000 @ $6.00	$96,000		
16,000 @ $12.00		$192,000	$192,000
LESS: COST OF G. S.	(68,000)	(96,000)	(68,000)
IMPORT CUSTOMS			
@ 15%		(14,400)	(14,400)
GROSS PROFIT	28,000	81,600	109,600
LESS: S & A EXPENSES	(10,300)	(75,000)	(85,300)
NET INCOME BEFORE TAX	17,700	6,600	24,300
LESS: INCOME TAX			
(30% & 50%)	(5,310)	(3,300)	(8,610)
NET INCOME	12,390	3,300	15,690

As a result of a $1.00 increase in the transfer price, tariffs to be paid to country B will be increased by $2,400 (15% of $16,000). Since the tax rate in country B is higher than in country A, the tax shield will be $1,200, plus the difference of avoiding paying 20% more of $16,000, which is $3,200. Therefore the global profits will be increased by $2,000. We can conclude from this analysis that as long as the tax rate differential (which is 20% in our case as the difference between the tax rates of the two countries) is higher than the net effect of tariff rates (which is 15% of the costs of goods transferred reduced by the tax shield of 50% of the 15% = 15% − 50% of 15% = 7.5%) imposed by the country with the higher tax rate, the higher transfer price will always generate net savings for the MNE (12.5% for each $1.00 increase in the transfer price per unit).

However, if the top management increases the price for goods transferred from subsidiary A to subsidiary B by $1.00 more (from $6.00 to $7.00), it will have a negative effect on both the global profits of the MNE and on the net income of subsidiary B, as can be seen from Table 3.3. For subsidiary A, the net income will be increased by $22,400, which is the increase in the transfer price after (16,000 units × [$7.00 − $5.00] = $32,000 × [1 − income tax rate in country B] 1 − 30% = $22,400).

For subsidiary B, the negative effect includes (1) an increase in costs of goods sold by $32,000 as a result of being charged a higher transfer price by $2.00 for 16,000 units, (2) an increase in tariffs paid on imports to country B ($4,800) at a 15% rate of the difference in the transfer price ($32,000), and (3) no income tax liability, since (1) and (2) will result in net loss before tax, and hence a reduction of income tax paid to the government of country B from $12,500 to zero. The net negative effect will be $32,000 + 4,800 − 12,500 = $24,300, a reduction in the net income of subsidiary B. The global net income will be decreased by $1,900, because the decrease in the net income of subsidiary B ($24,300) exceeds the increase in the net income of subsidiary A ($22,400). Therefore, if the transfer price goes over $6.00, as in the example illustrated in Table 3.3, the effect on the net income of both the transferee and the MNE as a whole will be detrimental. In general, the higher the import tariffs relative to the difference in net income tax rates between different countries, the more likely it is that a low transfer price is preferable.

In concluding this section, it is important to notice that there is a limit for any increase in the transfer price. When the higher transfer price results in showing a net loss for the buying subsidiary, the global profits of the MNE will decrease by the difference between the maximum tax savings the MNE could get, which is the tax shield of 50% of the increase in the cost of the goods transferred (50% of $32,000 = $16,000) plus the 50% tax shield of the increase in the tariffs (50% of $4,800 = $2,400), and the maximum tax reduction allowed (which is $12,500) because of achieving net loss and paying zero tax, assuming that there are no losses to be carried forward to the next year according to the tax regulations of country B. The net

Table 3.3
The Effect of Both Tax and Tariffs of High versus Low Transfer Prices

	A	B	THE GLOBE
LOW TRANSFER PRICE			
SALES			
16,000 @ 5.00	$80,000		
16,000 @ $12.00		$192,000	$192,000
LESS: COST OF G. S.	(68,000)	(80,000)	(68,000)
IMPORT CUSTOMS			
@ 15%		(12,000)	(12,000)
GROSS PROFIT	12,000	100,000	112,000
LESS: S, A, & G EXP.	(10,300)	(75,000)	(85,300)
NET INCOME BEFORE TAX	1,700	25,000	26,700
LESS: INCOME TAX			
(30% & 50%)	(510)	(12,500)	(13,010)
NET INCOME	1,190	12,500	13,690
HIGH TRANSFER PRICE:			
SALES			
16,000 @ $7.00	$112,000		
16,000 @ $12.00		$192,000	$192,000
LESS: COST OF G. S.	(68,000)	(112,000)	(68,000)
IMPORT CUSTOMS			
@ 15%		(16,800)	(16,800)
GROSS PROFIT	44,000	63,200	107,200
LESS: S, A, & G EXP.	(10,300)	(75,000)	(85,300)
NET INCOME BEFORE TAX	33,700	(11,800)	21,900
LESS: INCOME TAX			
(30% & 50%)	(10,110)	-0-	(10,110)
NET INCOME (LOSS)	23,590	(11,800)	11,790

effect, as indicated in the example, will be a $1,900 decrease in the global profits, resulting from paying more tariffs ($16,800 − $12,000 = $4,800) than tax savings of $2,900 ($13,010 − $10,110).

MINIMIZATION OF EXCHANGE RATE RISK

The risk of the foreign exchange rate arises from doing international business denominated in currencies other than the domestic currency. High fluctuations in foreign exchange rates cause high risk of loss or gain. International transfer prices may be used to reduce a MNE's foreign exchange risk, which is the risk of a gain or loss in the MNE's future economic value resulting from a change in the foreign exchange rates.[7]

Transfer pricing is one of the best means to be used to minimize foreign exchange losses from currency fluctuations or to shift the losses to another subsidiary by moving assets from one country to another under the floating exchange rates system. This can be done by determining what currency is to be used for payment and whether the buying or selling subsidiary has the foreign exchange risk. If this is done, the appropriate transfer price will have a significant effect on the net exposure of the subsidiary. In this case, funds in weak-currency countries are moved through the use of transfer pricing, especially when the foreign currency is not allowed to move out of the country.

As an example, let us assume that subsidiary A (an American subsidiary) sold $20,000 in merchandise in January 1986 to an Egyptian subsidiary and that the payment was in American dollars within 60 days, at a time when the exchange rate was U.S. $1 = 1 Egyptian pound (EP). Let us also assume that the MNE headquarters imposed a transfer price of $22,000. The American subsidiary would receive $2,000 (or EP 2,000) more, but the assets of the Egyptian subsidiary would have been reduced by EP 2,000 or $2,000. The difference in the price does not affect the global profit of the MNE.

Funds in weak-currency countries can be siphoned off by using international transfer price adjustments. To use international transfer pricing effectively in gaining through the exchange rates, it must be coordinated with the currency-hedging techniques of "leading" or "lagging," which allow MNEs to avoid exchange risks and extract more funds out of a weak currency for conversion into a strong currency.[8]

At the time of payment, March 1986, if the exchange rate was $1.00 = EP 1.50, the Egyptian subsidiary had to pay the American subsidiary $22,000, which is equivalent to EP 33,000 at the time of payment. In this case, the MNE moved the profits from Egypt (which has a soft currency) to the U.S. currency. Subsidiary A, the American, received EP 11,000 more than the original transfer price and EP 2,000 more than the original market price. The result was EP 11,000 foreign exchange loss for the Egyptian subsidiary on a relatively small transaction.

Generally, assets in weak-currency countries are moved through the use of international transfer price adjustments. A MNE can change the transfer price to take advantage of expected movements in the exchange rate. This allows the MNE to charge high transfer prices when the currency is expected to decline. By doing so, it maintains the gross profit margins in terms of U.S. dollars, even though in local currencies the gross profit margin has increased. However, price controls or government intervention may limit the use of this technique.

AVOIDING A CONFLICT WITH HOST COUNTRIES' GOVERNMENTS

Transfer pricing policies of MNEs have a direct effect on countries' economies where they have foreign subsidiaries. MNEs need to set their transfer pricing policies to charge for goods and services transferred into and out of foreign countries on a basis that foreign governments will consider justified. To avoid a conflict with the host country's government, a MNE should not charge high transfer prices for any goods and services transferred, because high prices mean more cash or fund outflows from the country than cash inflows, which will have a direct impact on the country's balance of payments and consequently on its economy. Therefore, MNEs need to determine "what price" to charge for their own products manufactured in one country and transferred to another country to achieve reasonable global profits.

Foreign governments, on the other hand, especially in the third world countries, always concentrate on devising different tools, techniques, or regulations to minimize the effect of transfer pricing policies of MNEs on their countries. Host-country governments want to make sure that the long-term cash or fund outflows, such as dividends, royalties, and especially intracompany pricing manipulations, do not exceed significantly the value of goods, services, funds, or cash inflows.[9] Therefore, MNEs need to make a balance between maximizing their global profits by charging very high transfer prices and avoiding conflict with the host-country government by charging low transfer prices.

MANAGEMENT OF CASH FLOW

MNEs may need to withdraw funds from their foreign sub-sidiaries either because it is expected that a new political group is moving into the foreign government and an expropriation of most investments is anticipated, or because there are restrictions on moving cash out of the country due to balance of payments or exchange rate problems. International transfer pricing, dividends, royalties, and management service fees are the most important techniques for withdrawing cash from foreign countries. A MNE may raise transfer prices on goods or services transferred to a foreign subsidiary by another within the same organization by withdrawing funds from countries. Charging high transfer prices may be the only way to shift funds out of the country, as stated by an officer of a large MNE: "If I cannot get dividends out and my royalty rate is fixed, and I want to remit more money, then I do this on an uplift of my transfer prices."[10] Another officer indicated that his firms, even though they did not use transfer pricing for tax purposes, would push transfer prices up or down if exchange restrictions blocked the transfer of funds.[11]

COMPETITIVENESS IN THE FOREIGN MARKET

A MNE must help its foreign subsidiaries in their first stages of business in foreign countries. ITP systems can be used to help them in competition against other businesses by charging a low transfer price for goods shipped into those countries to keep these foreign subsidiaries competitive with other local businesses.

Competition can be in the final selling markets, the raw materials market, the intermediate market, or in the parent company's market.[12] However, a conflict may arise between foreign governments and MNEs that charge very low transfer prices for goods transferred into the country, expecially when there are import customs or duties imposed on the invoice price of goods, and/or the low transfer price helps foreign subsidiaries to compete against local firms and may drive them out of the market. In this case, foreign governments may intervene to protect their domestic industries and their tax or tariff revenues as well.

PERFORMANCE EVALUATION

MNEs set up their international transfer pricing policies at the central-management (or top-management) level to facilitate cash movements where currency restrictions exist and to minimize taxes. A conflict between international transfer pricing techniques and performance evaluation measurement is to be expected, and, in general, transfer pricing policies are not complementary to the profit-center concept.

The 1972 Committee on International Accounting of the American Accounting Association indicated that the traditional profit-center concept for performance evaluation is inappropriate for MNEs because there is no clear distinction between operating subdivisions of MNEs. With integrated, centrally coordinated operations, foreign subsidiary management does not have authority for major decisions that affect its reported profits.[13] The 1973 Committee on International Accounting of the American Accounting Association agreed with the previously reported conclusions and added that the differences between countries, such as social, economic, political, legal, and educational differences, have a considerable effect on a manager's performance. The committee concluded that there is a need for further research to introduce additional elements into traditional management accounting evaluation techniques.[14]

In evaluating the performance of the foreign subsidiary, it is appropriate to evaluate its contribution to the objectives and goals of the whole MNE. It is also important to evaluate the contribution of foreign subsidiary managers to the performance of the MNE. David Solomons has stated, "In the absence of evidence to the contrary, the presumption is that the success of one implies the success of the other. But circumstances outside a manager's control may dictate success or failure of the venture."[15]

The headquarters enforces a specific transfer price to be used by its own subsidiaries to achieve certain objectives such as domestic and foreign income tax minimization, foreign exchange risk reduction, and foreign exchange control avoidance, among others. To achieve these objectives, international transfer pricing may result in some foreign subsidiaries showing higher artificial profits, while others may show much lower artificial profits.

A foreign subsidiary manager may have the operations of his area being evaluated as if it were a completely autonomous and independent subsidiary. Managers may have the greatest degree of freedom in making decisions related to the short run. However, they have a lesser degree of freedom in making decisions directly affecting other foreign subsidiaries and the globe.

With the frequent fluctuations of currency values combined with the floating exchange rates system, MNEs face the problem of distorted performance measurements of their domestic and foreign subsidiaries as profit centers.[16] Performance of foreign subsidiaries in U.S.-based MNEs is usually evaluated on the basis of reports stated in U.S. dollars. However, as the exchange rates fluctuate, performance evaluation of subsidiaries is not an easy task. Using transfer pricing as a basis for performance evaluation under the floating exchange rates system is much more complicated because international transfer prices are not usually adjusted for any fluctuations in currency exchange rates.[17]

At Honeywell, Inc., Duane Malmstrom implemented a simple solution for this problem. His technique is called "dollar indexing." This technique is used to have the same impact as local currency invoicing, including two basic objectives: (1) to allow realistic performance evaluation, and (2) to reflect the real economic cost of the product transferred.[18] Malmstrom used an indexed formula for U.S.-dollar transfer prices:

$$NTP = OTP \times \frac{CER}{PER}$$

where

NTP = New transfer price

OTP = Old transfer price

CER = Current exchange rate

PER = Planned exchange rate

Using this formula will result in applying a uniform transfer price for all goods transferred out of the same subsidiary.

For illustration, let us assume that subsidiary A in the United Kingdom transferred 16,000 units of its products at a transfer price established by the parent U.S.-based MNE at $5.00 per unit to another foreign subsidiary B in Switzerland owned by the same MNE. The foreign exchange rates were £1.00 = $1.63 and Swiss franc (SF) 1.00 = $1.49 respectively. As can be seen in Table 3.4, subsidiary A achieves a net income of $6,700 or £4,110 (in the British currency), while subsidiary B achieves a net income of $37,000, or 24,832 in Swiss francs.

If we assume that the U.S. dollar was depreciated equally against both the British and the Swiss currencies to £1.00 = $2.188 and SF 1 = $2.00 respectively, the income statements for both subsidiaries and the MNE measured in U.S. dollars and local currencies would be as shown in Table 3.5. Since the transfer price ($5.00 per unit) was set centrally by the U.S.-based MNE, the operating results of the British subsidiary would show a net loss of $18,394 or £8,407, while the Swiss subsidiary would achieve a net income of $77,046 or SF 38,523 because of the devaluation of the U.S. dollar in the international markets.

The effect of using the $5.00 as a transfer price for international operations when there was devaluation in the parent's currency resulted in switching the operating results of the selling subsidiary from net income of 8% of sales to a net loss of 23% of sales. On the other hand, the operating results of the buying subsidiary would be in the opposite direction, switching from a net income of 19% to a higher net income of 30%. That is, this transaction not only transferred goods from the British subsidiary to the Swiss subsidiary but also transferred $25,094 ($6,700 + $18,394) of profits and a translation gain of $14,952, a total of $40,042. In this case, the MNE as a whole should show a profit $14,952 higher than before because of the translation gain resulting from the devaluation of the U.S. dollar. For performance evaluation purposes, the manager of the British subsidiary was negatively affected by the change in the exchange rate and the imposed transfer price, while the Swiss subsidiary's manager did nothing more than before but showed a 30% net income percentage (11% higher than before the change occurred).

Using the indexed formula for U.S.-dollar transfer prices suggested by Malmstrom, the adjusted transfer price would be

$$NTP = OTP \times \frac{CER}{PER}$$

$$NTP = \$5.00 \times \frac{£2.188}{£1.630} = \$6.71$$

Table 3.4
The Effect of Transfer Pricing on Performance Evaluation

	SUBSIDIARY A (SELLER)		SUBSIDIARY B (BUYER)		THE GLOBAL INCOME
	US$	UK	US$	SF	STATEMENT, US$
SALES					
16,000 @ $5.00	$80,000	£49,080			
16,000 @ $12.00			$192,000	SF 128,859	$192,000
LESS: COST OF G. S.	(68,000)	41,718	(80,000)	(53,691)	(68,000)
GROSS PROFIT	12,000	7,362	112,000	75,168	124,000
LESS: S, A, & G EXP.	(5,300)	(3,252)	(75,000)	(50,336)	(80,300)
NET INCOME BEFORE TAX	6,700	4,110	37,000	24,832	43,700
NET INCOME AS A PERCENTAGE OF SALES	8%	8%	19%	19%	22.8%

Table 3.5
The Effect of Transfer Pricing with Changes in Foreign Exchange Rates on Performance Evaluation

SALES	$80,000	£36,563	$257,718	SF 128,859	$257,718
16,000 @ $5.00					
LESS: COST OF G. S.	(91,279)	(41,718)	(80,000)	(40,000)	(91,279)
GROSS PROFIT	(11,279)	(5,155)	177,718	88,859	166,439
LESS S, A, & G EXP.	(7,115)	(3,252)	(100,672)	(50,336)	(107,787)
NET INCOME BEFORE TAX	(18,394)	(8,407)	77,046	38,523	58,652
NET INCOME AS A PERCENTAGE OF SALES	(23%)	(23%)	30%	30%	22.8%

or

$$NTP = \$5.00 \times \frac{SF\ 2.00}{SF\ 1.49} = \$6.71$$

Table 3.6 shows the effect of transfer prices adjusted for changes in exchange rates. The new transfer price is $6.71, which is higher than the old one. For subsidiaries A and B, the net income percentage as related to sales is the same as before any changes in the exchange rate, and both

Table 3.6
The Effect of Transfer Prices Adjusted for Changes in Exchange Rates

	SUBSIDIARY A		SUBSIDIARY B		THE GLOBAL RESULTS
	US$	UK	US$	SF	US$
SALES					
(16,000 @ $6.71)	$107,360	£49,068	$257,718	SF 128,859	$257,718
LESS: COST OF G. S.	(91,279)	(41,718)	(107,360)	(53,691)	(91,279)
GROSS PROFITS	16,081	7,350	150,358	75,168	166,439
LESS: S ,A & G					
EXPENSES	(7,115)	(3,253)	(100,672)	(50,336)	(107,787)
NET INCOME	8,966	4,098	49,686	24,832	58,652
NET INCOME AS A PERCEMTAGE OF OF SALES	8%	8%	19%	19%	22.8%

EXCHANGE RATES:

  £ 1.00= $2.188 US$
  SF 1.00= $2.00 US$

THE NEW TRANSFER PRICE (ADJUSTED FOR FOREIGN CURRENCY
  FLUCTUATIONS) = $6.71

of them had the same measured performance as before. The MNE
had higher global profits with the dollar devaluation by $14,952,
which is a translation gain. However, the translation gains were
divided in such a way that the Swiss subsidiary received $12,686 out
of total translation gains of $14,952, while the British subsidiary
received only $2,266 due to how much the U.S. dollar was devalued
in relation to the local currency. In other words, Malmstrom's system
does not work as it should; it still gives distorted financial results
because of the foreign currency fluctuations.

MOTIVATION

Motivation is considered as one of the objectives of setting an international transfer pricing policy for domestic and foreign subsidiaries. Subsidiary managers need to be motivated to maximize (or

increase) their divisional profits and transfer their products or services in and out of their areas of responsibility within the MNE at appropriate transfer prices. Transfer prices, in this case, can be used to motivate subsidiary managers to achieve their divisional goals (by maximizing their divisional profits) and at the same time achieving their MNE's goals (by maximizing the global profits).

However, the more autonomy subsidiary managers have to decide on their transfer pricing to achieve their divisional profits, the more conflict may exist between achieving MNE and divisional profits. Conflicts may also arise between different objectives of using transfer pricing policies. Higher transfer pricing for intracompany sales may help subsidiary managers to show higher profits and be more motivated by making their best efforts to achieve the MNE's goal. However, if the tax rate of the foreign country where a subsidiary is located is very high, the global profits will be decreased, and a conflict of goal congruence will exist between divisional goals and global goals.

For an international transfer pricing system to be a motivator, it must be tied to performance of subsidiary managers. In order to be used as a measure of performance, an international transfer pricing system must meet the following four criteria:[19]

1. It must be a result of the manager's behavior.
2. It must include all the actions that need to be performed.
3. It must be accepted by subsidiary managers as a valid measurement of their performance.
4. It must include attainable goals for subsidiary managers.

Does the transfer price measure completely the foreign subsidiary manager's performance? That is, does the transfer pricing system reflect all the actions that should be performed by the foreign subsidiary manager in selling his products to another subsidiary? Certainly the answer is no, because a foreign subsidiary manager does not have control over the fluctuations of the exchange rate of the foreign currency of the country in which he is doing business. He can easily achieve translation gains or losses to be included in his performance report because of political, legal, economic, or social factors over which he does not have any degree of control. His profits can go up or down because of sudden increases in inflation rates and/or commodity or stock prices, and the outcome will be an increase or decrease in the market price when it is used as a transfer price.

MNEs must analyze the potential impact of using a transfer pricing system as a motivator on foreign subsidiary managers' performance. Actions or decisions that are made by managers to improve their performance can have a negative effect on the global goals or profits of the MNE as a whole. Whenever international transfer pricing objectives lead to conflicting consequences, MNEs are forced into trade-offs between achieving different objectives and must accept lower global profits when one objective has a priority over others, especially for achieving long-term objectives.

GOAL CONGRUENCE

Goal congruence exists when the goals of the MNE's subsidiary managers, so far as feasible, are consistent with the global goals of the MNE. In establishing an ITP policy, top management would like to motivate subsidiary managers to achieve the subsidiary's goals by contributing toward the achievement of the MNE's goals. It is almost impossible to achieve perfect congruence between subsidiary managers' goals and the MNE's goals. However, at least the ITP policies should not motivate subsidiary managers to make decisions that may be in conflict with the MNE's goals.

Motivation and goal congruence are important factors in designing ITP sytems. If a MNE desires to have its subsidiary manager strongly motivated toward achieving congruent goals, it is necessary to consider the effect of the transfer pricing on their divisional profitability or performance. However, if there is a conflict between subsidiary managers' goals and the global goals, it may be preferable to have as little motivation and autonomy of subsidiary managers as possible.

Generally, an ITP system should be designed in such a way that a foreign or domestic subsidiary manager is motivated to make decisions that are in the best interest of the MNE as a whole. When subsidiary managers increase their divisional profits and at the same time increase the global profits, then subsidiary managers are in the MNE's interest if the ITP system does not mislead managers about what the MNE's interests really are. However, both subsidiary managers and central management must be aware that the measurement of the subsidiary's net income (or contribution) under this ITP system is inherently imperfect, and the limited usefulness of that performance measure is further complicated by the existence of common resources used within the MNE.

SUMMARY AND CONCLUSION

This chapter has identified and discussed nine different objectives of establishing an international transfer pricing policy: (1) reduction of income taxes, (2) reduction of tariffs, (3) minimization of foreign exchange risks, (4) avoidance of a conflict with host countries' governments, (5) management of cash flows, (6) competitiveness, (7) performance evaluation, (8) motivation, and (9) goal congruence. For the first two objectives combined, as long as the tax rate differential is higher than the net effect of the tariff rate imposed by the country with the higher tax rate, the higher transfer price will always generate net savings for the MNE. However, if the higher transfer price results in showing artificial losses for the buying subsidiary, the net effect will be detrimental for the MNE as a whole.

With the fluctuations in foreign exchange rates, assets in weak currencies can be moved through the use of higher transfer prices. However, host-government intervention with or without price controls will certainly limit the MNE's use of this technique. When performance evaluation systems combine with fluctuations in foreign exchange rates, transfer pricing policies will lead to misleading and imperfect financial measures of performance. Malmstrom's system (dollar-indexing technique) has been believed to give distorted financial results for performance evaluation.

Motivation, goal congruence, and autonomy of foreign subsidiaries and their managers always lead to conflicting results with performance evaluation, reduction of income taxes, reduction of tariffs, and avoidance of foreign exchange risks. However, when different objectives lead to conficting consequences, MNEs have to make trade-offs between achieving different objectives and must be satisfied with lower global profits when one objective has a priority over others, especially for achieving long-term objectives.

In designing an international transfer pricing policy, business literature, especially accounting, does not provide MNEs with any unique technique or model to help them arrive at the appropriate transfer price. Therefore, MNEs are in urgent need of a practical and objective technique or model that can avoid conflicts between different objectives of the system and, at the same time, achieve the global goals of MNEs to continue doing their international business under different political, economic, and social environmental conditions.

NOTES

1. Alan M. Rugman, "Internationalization Theory and Corporate International Finance," *California Management Review* (Winter 1980): 76.

2. Lynette L. Knowles and Ike Mathur, "International Transfer Pricing Objectives," *Managerial Finance* 11 (1985): 12.

3. C. R. Greenhill and E. O. Herbalzheimer, "International Transfer Pricing: The Restructive Business Practices Approach," *Journal of World Trade Law* (May–June 1980): 232.

4. Ibid.

5. Ralph L. Benke, Jr., and James Don Edwards, *Transfer Pricing Techniques and Uses* (New York: National Association of Accountants, 1980), 114.

6. H. Seung Kim and Stephen W. Miller, "Constituents of the International Transfer Pricing Decisions," *Columbia Journal of World Business* (Spring 1979): 71.

7. Lars Oxelheim, *International Financial Market Fluctuations* (New York: John Wiley and Sons, 1985), 61.

8. Sylvain R. F. Plosschaert, "The Multiple Motivations for Transfer Pricing Modulations in Multinational Enterprises and Governmental Counter Measures: An Attempt at Clarification," *Management International Review* (1981/1): 49–63.

9. L. le Van Hall, "The Multinational Corporation: Its Impact on Developing Countries," in *The Multinational Corporation: Accounting and Social Implications*," (Urbana: Center for International Education and Research in Accounting, University of Illinois, 1977), 94.

10. Sidney M. Robbins and Robert B. Stobaugh, *Money in the Multinational Enterprise* (New York: Basic Books, 1973): 91.

11. Ibid.

12. Jeffrey S. Arpan, *International Intracompany Pricing: Non American Systems and Views* (New York: Praeger Publishers, 1972), 70.

13. *An Introduction to Financial Control and Reporting in Multinational Enterprise* (Austin, Bureau of Business Research, University of Texas at Austin, 1973), 71–73.

14. American Accounting Association, "Report of the Committee on International Accounting," *Accounting Review* 49 (1974 Supplement): 252–57.

15. David Solomons, *Divisional Performance: Measurement and Control* (Homewood, Ill.: Richard D. Irwin, 1965), 59.

16. Duane Malmstrom, "Accommodating Exchange Rate Fluctuations in Intercompany Pricing and Invoicing," *Management Accounting* (September 1977): 25.

17. Benke and Edwards, *Transfer Pricing Techniques and Uses*, 118.

18. Malmstrom, "Accommodating Exchange Rate Fluctuations," 25.

19. Edward Lawler, *Motivation in Work Organizations* (Belmont: Calif.: Wadsworth Publishing Company, 1973), 133.

4

International Transfer Pricing Techniques

MNEs use transfer pricing policies as a way to achieve certain objectives. Two sets of objectives known in business literature are internal and external. Internally, MNEs use transfer prices in the accounting sense as accounting prices, to account for transactions between different subsidiaries within the same organization. They are also used for decision making on the allocation of resources between different subsidiaries, and to help top management manage a decentralized organization by integrating and coordinating autonomous (or pseudo-autonomous) subsidiaries all over the world. Motivation, control, and performance evaluation of subsidiaries within MNEs are other objectives for using transfer prices. At the top of the objectives stands goal congruence, which requires that all actions and decisions made by subsidiary managers be in the best interest of the MNE as a whole.

The second set of objectives relates to factors outside the home country. From the viewpoint of a MNE, transfer prices are used to allocate net income among different subsidiaries in different countries under different legal, social, and economic regulations. Externally, MNEs face other problems, such as different income tax rates of different countries, tax structures and requirements, quotas and import duties, cash movement restrictions, currency exchange control, and conflicts with host governments. From the viewpoint of the United States or any other foreign government, transfer pricing policies create problems because of the belief that they do not reflect open market prices.[1] Governments believe also that MNEs set their own transfer pricing policies to avoid paying taxes. Therefore MNEs are in conflict with both home and host governments.[2]

The two sets of objectives are not directly related to each other, and there is no evidence that any single transfer price designed for only one of these objectives will satisfy all others. No practical evidence has been found concerning the appropriate (or optimal) transfer price for a MNE to use. There are three reasons for this problem.

First, changing environmental conditions, such as market conditions, government attitudes, and different global strategies, force MNEs to use different transfer prices at different times under different environmental conditions. Second, balance of payments, tax revenues, and market structures of different countries, among other factors, are affected by the use of transfer prices. There is no easy way to "ascertain ex post whether a given transfer price level was practiced ex ante with a view to minimize taxes or regulations or primarily on business grounds."[3] Third, if the transfer price does not reflect the market conditions or if it deviates from the arm's-length price between unaffiliated companies, then it is unacceptable. "The extent of the deviation depends on the yardstick used; . . . the implementation of the yardstick is difficult and frequently gets enmeshed in the issue of the fair price, whatever that concept may mean."[4]

To choose the appropriate transfer pricing policy, it is essential to look at what has been discussed in business literature on transfer pricing policies from both theory and practice. Transfer pricing methods can be divided into four groups: (1) economic and accounting-oriented analysis, (2) mathematically oriented analysis (including linear and nonlinear models), and (3) empirical studies based on questionnaires and/or interview surveys. Within these groups, most of the articles discuss the theoretical side to justify using one technique for transfer pricing over others. Empirical studies were limited in their findings because of their limited data obtained by means of subjective questionnaires or personal interviews.

ECONOMIC AND ACCOUNTING-ORIENTED ANALYSIS

The economic and accounting-oriented techniques fall into one of the following subgroups: (a) market price; (b) cost-based and cost-plus methods, including full production cost, full production cost plus profit margin, variable production cost, and variable production cost plus profit margin; (c) marginal cost-based and (d) negotiated price.

Market Price

The market price is the price that prevails when a manufacturing subsidiary sells its products to an external customer; that is, the manufacturing subsidiary charges the same price to the buying subsidiary as it would charge an external customer in arm's-length transactions. However, there are four criteria that should be satisfied to use the market price as a transfer price: (1) there exists a competitive intermediate market; (2) subsidiary managers have freedom in decision making; that is, they can decide either to buy or sell internally or in the open market without any interference of top management; (3) subsidiary managers have their own autonomy or at least a minimal degree of interdependence among profit centers; and (4) there is a known market price that can be quoted anytime.

There are several advantages to using the market price. First, if a market price can be determined, it is the best price to be used for performance evaluation of the profit centers, since it motivates managers to act as if they were managing their own business and consequently reduces costs of production and increases their divisional profits. Second, market prices correspond to the arm's-length price, and MNEs can avoid any conflict with either home- or host-country governments. Third, subsidiary managers, especially in foreign countries, may be well qualified to make quick decisions under certain circumstances to avoid any negative consequences from interference by the government.

There are, however, some problems that may result from using market prices. First, the appropriate market price may be difficult to determine. It may be different from one country to another even if it is in the same currency, or it may be different from time to time. Therefore, market price may be difficult to establish. Second, in the international market, transportation costs are signifiant and are different from one location to another. That makes it impossible to have a uniform market price for the same product of the same MNE that is sold in different countries. Third, supply and demand in foreign markets requires establishing a price that will prevail in that market and will help foreign subsidiaries to compete with other subsidiaries. Therefore, there is no unique market price to be quoted.

Cost-Based and Cost-Plus Methods

Cost-based transfer pricing may be used when market prices do not exist or are not available for MNEs to use for international transfer pricing. Under cost-based methods, cost may mean different things and have different effects on performance evaluation, motivation, decision making, divisional profits, income tax liability, and global profits.

Cost-based methods include full cost (actual or standard) and variable cost (actual or standard). Standard or budgeted costs are preferred over actual costs, because they encourage MNEs to control the cost efficiency of their domestic and foreign subsidiaries. Full cost includes direct material, direct labor, and factory overhead. It offers three major advantages: (1) availability of cost information is provided by the accounting system currently in use by the MNE, (2) it is also in conformity with U.S. generally accepted accounting principles concerning inventory valuation and income determination, and (3) it may motivate foreign subsidiary managers to increase their divisional contribution as long as the full absorption cost exceeds the variable cost and there is additional capacity to accommodate the incoming orders.

However, the use of the full absorption costing method can create many problems, which can be summarized as follows:

1. If the selling subsidiary is assured of covering all full production costs on all goods transferred internally, there is little incentive for foreign subsidiary managers to have control over their divisional costs, to produce efficiently, or to make rational decisions related to their area of responsibilities as long as the cost of their inefficient use of resources is passed on to the buying subsidiaries. This can be avoided by using standard costs rather than actual costs for transfer pricing.

2. If the full cost exceeds the market price, the buying subsidiary manager would be motivated to buy from the market outside the MNE and consequently would create idle capacity for the MNE as a whole.

3. This method leads to suboptimal short-run decisions for the MNE as a whole when the buying subsidiary treats the fixed costs of the selling subsidiary as variable costs.

A variable cost-based transfer price leads the buying subsidiary to make optimal decisions in the best interest from the MNE viewpoint. The MNE's variable costs (either actual or standard) are considered as the buying subsidiary's variable costs as it acts in the international market. However, using the variable cost-based transfer price forces the selling subsidiary to report zero profit or a loss equal to its fixed costs.

For making long-run pricing decisions, variable cost-based transfer pricing will mislead the buying subsidiary managers in making the appropriate pricing decisions to compete in the international market from the MNE viewpoint. In other words, the subsidiary manager's decision may not be in the best interest of the MNE as a whole.

Cost-plus transfer pricing may use actual or standard costs which should be marked up to allow the selling subsidiary to realize a profit. A markup can be a flat percentage of the cost (actual, standard, full, or variable). It should allow the foreign subsidiary to recover its normal operating costs plus an appropriate markup to earn a return on investment equal to that earned in the domestic market.[5]

A major reason for the common use of cost-plus transfer pricing is its simplicity, clarity, and its approximation of the market price, especially when the intermediate product has an international market. It is also a justifiable and reasonable transfer price when there is no market for the product. However, it may lead to suboptimal decisions for the MNE as a whole when it is not related to some economic reality.[6]

Marginal Cost-Based Method

Marginal cost is the change in total cost that results from an increase in production by one unit. Under the marginal cost-based method, the transfer price is to be set at the marginal cost of the selling subsidiary. The selling subsidiary should produce when its marginal cost (the transfer price) is equal to its marginal revenue, which will lead to maximization of the profits of the MNE. The marginal cost-based transfer pricing is presumed to result in an optimal production for the MNE.

The marginal cost-based method is appropriate when there is neither an external market for the intermediate product nor an agreeable negotiated transfer price between the two subsidiaries. However, information on marginal cost cannot be practically collected from the MNE accounting system. Several empirical studies showed that marginal transfer pricing, which is a theoretical technique, is unrealistic and of very little use in practice.[7]

Negotiated Transfer Pricing Method

A negotiated transfer price is used when the buying and the selling subsidiaries are free to negotiate the acceptable transfer price for both of them. This method retains the independence of each manager to make the right decision for his subsidiary and makes each manager accountable for the outcome of his decisions. Therefore, it motivates subsidiary managers to have control over their costs and increase their divisional contribution to the MNE.

However, it may lead to suboptimal decisions, especially when the final product is sold in a different country and other factors, such as different tax rates, different government regulations, different tariffs, and competition, are ignored. Another problem is that negotiations may need too much time; this is a time-consuming process and may require top-management intervention for settlement.

MATHEMATICALLY ORIENTED ANALYSIS

Mathematical programming techniques were introduced after the failure of the traditional economic models to solve transfer pricing problems. The mathematical programming models allocate the resources efficiently and, at the same time, evaluate the efficient use of the resources under a decentralized organization.[8] These techniques are (a) linear programming models, which deal with allocation problems in which the objective (or goal) and all the requirements imposed are expressed by linear functions; (b) nonlinear programming models, which are used when the goal and/or one or more of the requirements imposed are expressed by nonlinear functions; and (c) a goal-programming model, which is used when there are multiple goals for a MNE. Under all these techniques, a mathematical model sets transfer prices at the opportunity costs (or the shadow prices) of the intermediate product.

However, the suggested mathematical programming techniques have the following drawbacks:

1. The MNE must obtain suboptimal divisional information in order to maintain "efficient decentralized operations".[9] When transfer prices are set centrally, the autonomy of foreign subsidiary managers is ignored completely, and the profit-center concept is not applicable under these conditions.

2. The existence of different economic, political, and social variables may require setting a different transfer price in each country where

a foreign subsidiary is located. In other words, different tax rates, foreign exchange risks, expropriation risks, government interventions, and avoiding any conflicts with host-country governments are just examples of many problems that MNEs face in doing business abroad, and they may make the development of any mathematical programming model for MNEs much more difficult than for domestic firms, if not impossible. Therefore, experimental or empirical studies are badly needed to validate the use of these models within MNEs.

3. These models do not give any consideration to the behavioral implications of using transfer pricing; therefore, they do not achieve the objectives of establishing international transfer pricing.

4. In evaluating the managers' performance as one of the objectives of international transfer pricing policies within these models, performance evaluation is assumed to be a function of profits. However, performance evaluation may be affected by divisional costs, variances between budgeted and actual costs, or any other factors that should be incorporated into the system.[10]

EMPIRICAL STUDIES

An investigation of the literature on transfer pricing indicated that little research has been done to develop a practical model on transfer pricing policies that can help MNEs and their subsidiary managers to solve all problems caused by intracompany transactions. Most academicians and practitioners have gone only as far as describing transfer pricing methods used by both domestic and international firms by means of interview surveys or subjective questionnaires. For instance, the National Industrial Conference Board in 1970 discussed, summarized, and presented the main business factors that affect the transfer pricing decisions of MNEs.[11]

In 1972 Jeffrey Arpan surveyed the transfer pricing systems in non-U.S. MNEs. He concluded that the transfer pricing policies of the non-U.S. MNEs are generally less complex and more market oriented than those of American MNEs. He also noted that U.S., British, Japanese, and French managers prefer the use of cost-oriented methods, while Canadians, Italians, and Scandinavians prefer the use of market prices.[12]

In 1979 H. Seung Kim and Stephen W. Miller used survey data and personal interviews with international business practitioners and suggested that the use of transfer pricing policies should be compatible with the long-run objectives of the firm. They also came to the conclusion that avoiding the restrictions on exchange control and profit repatriation, not avoiding income tax liabilities, is the major factor affecting the establishment of transfer pricing policies by U.S. MNEs, especially in developing countries.[13] Finally, Ralph Benke and James Don Edwards interviewed different officers of American companies, described several transfer pricing techniques currently used by American MNEs, and suggested the use of a single transfer price including lost contribution margin, which was called the opportunity cost.[14]

Tables 4.1 and 4.2 summarize the results of different empirical studies of international transfer pricing methods used by American, Canadian, Japanese, and British MNEs. The market price method was the one generally used by most of the American and Canadian MNEs for transfer pricing policies. The full cost plus a profit margin was ranked as the one most used by MNEs in the United States when there is no market price available and by the Japanese MNEs. The negotiated price was ranked the first for the British MNEs. For MNEs using cost-based methods, standard costs are more widely used than actual costs by American MNEs.

The general conclusions that can be drawn from the empirical survey literature are the following:

1. MNEs use more than one transfer price for their intracompany transactions. However, the market price is the most important transfer pricing method, followed by standard unit variable cost plus a profit margin.

2. Empirical studies indicate that the global strategy of MNEs, exchange control, income tax liability, and performance evaluation are the key factors in deciding what transfer pricing method to use.

3. From a MNE's viewpoint, accounting information is not the only input for the decision-making process. Other important factors to be considered include overall MNE objectives, global strategy, and the environmental conditions in both the United States and abroad.

4. MNEs know how to manipulate their transfer prices to achieve their goals. However, they are aware that doing so may open the door for government interventions, repatriation, and unlimited long-run deteriorations of their global objectives.

Table 4.1
The Results of Empirical Studies on the Use of International Transfer Pricing Techniques by MNEs

	American		Japanese	Canadian	British
Methods	Eccles	Tang, Walter, and Raymond	Tang, Walter, and Raymond	Tang	Tang
Market Price	30.0%	20.4%	22.2%	26.9%	23.9%
Cost-Based					
Variable	4.5%	0.81%	1.6%	2.7%	
Full Cost	24.7%	10.2%	4.8%	6.5%	7.0%
Cost-Plus	16.2%				
Variable Cost-Plus		1.7%	1.6%	2.8%	2.8%
Full Cost-Plus		32.2%	33.3%	19.4%	22.6%
Negotiated price	21.5%	13.6%	22.2%	25.9%	26.8%
Others	3.2%	21.1%	14.3%	15.81%	16.9%
	100.0%	100.0%	100.0%	100.00%	100.0%

Sources: Robert G. Eccles, The Transfer Pricing Problem: A Theory for Pactice (Lexington, Mass.: Lexington Books, 1985); Roger Y. W. Tang, C. K. Walter, and Robert H. Raymond, "Transfer Pricing: Japanese vs. American Style," Management Accounting (January, 1979): 12-16; Roger Y. W. Tang, Multinational Transfer Pricing: Canadian and British Perspectives (Toronto: Butterworth and Co. 1981).

SUMMARY AND CONCLUSIONS

The objective of an appropriate ITP technique for either internal reporting, external reporting, or both is determined largely by the objectives of establishing an ITP policy. Transfer pricing methods are divided into two groups: (1) economic and accounting-oriented analysis includes the market price, cost-based, cost-plus, marginal cost-based, and negotiated price methods; and (2) mathematically oriented analysis includes linear, nonlinear, and goal-programming models.

Table 4.2
The Ranking of International Transfer Pricing Methods Used by U.S.-Based MNEs

METHODS	Market Price available	Market Price unavailable	Yunker
Market Price	1.0		1.0
Adjusted Market Price	4.0		3.0
Variable Cost	7.0	5.5	
Standard			11.0
Actual			12.0
Full Market Cost	5.0	3.0	
Standard			7.0
Actual			8.0
Full Product Cost Plus Profit	2.0	1.0	
Standard			2.0
Actual			5.0
Variable Cost Plus Profit	8.0	5.5	
Standard			9.0
Actual			10.0
Negotiated Price	3.0	2.0	4.0
Others			
Linear Programming Techniques	9.0	7.0	
Marginal Cost	6.0	4.0	
Case-by-Case basis			6.0
Contribution Margin			13.0
Dual Pricing			14.0

Sources: Frederick H. Wu and Douglas Sharp, "An Empirical Study of Transfer Pricing Practice," The International Journal of Accounting (Spring, 1979): 71-99 (market Prices); Penelope J. Yunker, "A Survey Study of Subsidiary Autonomy, Performance Evaluation, and Transfer Pricing in Multinational Corporations," Columbia Journal of World Business (Fall 1983): 51-64.

A technique or method useful for one group of objectives or for one purpose may not be the best choice for another. The two sets of objectives discussed in this chapter are not directly related to each other, and there is no evidence that any single transfer price designed for only one of the ITP objectives will satisfy all others. No practical evidence has been found concerning the appropriate (or optimal) transfer price for MNEs to use. There are many reasons for this conclusion:

1. The significance of and fast changes in environmental conditions, such as market conditions, government attitudes, and differential global strategies, force MNEs to use different transfer prices at different times under different conditions.

2. Home and host countries' balance of payments, tax revenues, and market structures, among other factors, are affected by the use of transfer pricing policies.

3. The use of any transfer price other than the arm's-length price is unacceptable to tax authorities.

4. Foreign exchange risks, expropriation risks, government interventions, and avoiding any conflict with host countries' governments are just examples of many problems that face MNEs in developing an appropriate ITP policy and make it much more difficult than for domestic firms, if not impossible.

5. Empirical studies have indicated that the key factors in deciding what transfer pricing method to use are the global strategy of MNEs, exchange controls, income tax liability, and performance enduration.

NOTES

1. Alan M. Rugman and Lorraine Eden, "Introduction," in *Multinationals and Transfer Pricing* (New York: Saint Martin's Press, 1985), 1.

2. Ibid.

3. Sylvain R. F. Plasschaert, *Transfer Pricing and Multinational Corporations: An Overview of Concepts, Mechanisms, and Regulations* (New York: Praeger Publishers, 1979), 12.

4. Ibid.

5. Richard J. Nagy, "Transfer Price Accounting for MNEs," *Management Accounting* (January 1987): 35.

6. Ralph L. Benke, Jr., and James Don Edwards, *Transfer Pricing Techniques and Uses* (New York: National Association of Accountants, 1985), 65.

7. Ibid., 64.

8. For details, see A. Rashad Abdel-Khalik and Edward J. Lusk, "Transfer Pricing: A Synthesis," *Accounting Review* 69 (January, 1974), 15–17, and W. J. Baumal and T. Fabian, "Decomposition, Pricing for Decentralization, and External Economies," *Management Science* (1964): 1–32.

9. Andrew D. Bailey, Jr., and Warren J. Boe, "Goal and Resource Transfers in the Multigoal Organization," *Accounting Review* 51 (July 1976): 561.

10. Abdel-Kahlik and Lusk, "Transfer Pricing," 20.

11. James Greene and Michael D. Duerr, *Inter Company Transactions in the Multinational Firm: A Survey* (National Industrial Conference Board, New York, 1970), 1–2.

12. See Jeffrey S. Arpan, *International Intracompany Pricing: Non American Systems and Views* (New York: Praeger Publishers, 1971).

13. H. Seung Kim and Stephen W. Miller, "Constituents of the International Transfer Pricing Decisions," *Columbia Journal of World Business* (Spring 1979): 69–77.

14. See Benke and Edwards, *Transfer Pricing Techniques and Uses.*

5

International Transfer Pricing Policies and Managerial Decision Making in MNEs

Decision making is an integral part of both a MNE's subsidiary managers and its top management. It involves a choice between two or more available methods or techniques of transfer pricing after an evaluation of these methods, their impact on different internal and external factors, and the likelihood of progress toward achieving divisional objectives with a minimum degree of conflict with the MNE's long-term policies and objectives.

In a MNE each subsidiary manager is responsible for a choice between different transfer prices. A problem may arise when managers of both buying and selling subsidiaries, faced with a decision, cannot arrive at an agreed transfer price to achieve both their divisional objectives and the global objectives of the MNE.

However, for a MNE to know how effective its international transfer pricing system is, the following two questions can be asked: Does the system achieve economic decisions that positively affect MNE performance, including international capital investment decisions, output-level decisions for both intermediate and final products, and product pricing decisions for external customers? And do subsidiary managers feel that they are being fairly evaluated and rewarded for their divisional contributions to the MNE as a whole? If they do not, there may be short- and long-term negative effects on global profits of the MNE.[1]

There are many different types of management decisions, and each one may need a different method of transfer pricing techniques. The five most widely used managerial decisions with transfer pricing policies are (*a*) capital investment budgeting decisions, (*b*) the decision of whether to manufacture a product internally and transfer it to other foreign subsidiaries or to purchase it from the external international market, (*c*) product pricing decisions for the external customers of both intermediate and final products, (*d*) output-level decisions for both the intermediate and the final products, and (*e*) the use of transfer pricing to make the MNE's strategic decisions. Because of limited space only capital budgeting decisions will be discussed in this book.

CAPITAL BUDGETING DECISIONS

Making capital investment decisions is the process by which a MNE chooses the most profitable investments after considering different options and risks of domestic and foreign projects. Capital investment decisions about foreign investments are more complicated than domestic ones because of the existence of unique and different problems that are not faced by domestic enterprises.

Capital investment in the international market requires familiarity with foreign economic, political, and legal environmental conditions. MNEs need more relevant techniques or models for international capital budgeting decisions that must include the effects of all environmental variables and their impact on the global profits of MNEs.

Several environmental variables must be considered in the international capital budgeting decisions as compared to the domestic ones. These variables include the following:

1. Cash flows from foreign projects or subsidiaries must be differentiated from cash flows from the parent.
2. Differential tax systems, regulations, duties, and tariffs are essential in projecting any changes in cash flows.
3. Expectations of future movements of foreign exchange rates and inflation rates may affect profitability and the competitive position of a foreign subsidiary and the value of its cash flows to the parent.
4. Remittance of funds policies, such as limitations on remittance of dividends, technical fees, and royalties, of foreign countries must be

recognized because they are critical in achieving the rate of return on investment as measured by the net annual cash inflows realized on the investment basis.

5. Political, financial, environmental, and business risks are impor- tant in predicting the reaction of the present or future government to the capital investment and any anticipated restrictions on cash flows that may affect the value of a capital investment in a foreign country. Also, the risk of expropriation needs to be considered and evaluated.

A transfer pricing policy is considered to be an important input factor in capital budgeting decisions, as can be seen in Figure 5.1. In the five environmental variables mentioned earlier, transfer pricing policy is an integral part of each of the following three issues. First, it is essential to know how much a MNE may withdraw funds from its foreign investment; this is the cash flow from the project. Transfer pricing, dividends, royalties, and management service fees are the only techniques to withdraw cash from foreign investments where there are government restrictions on cash outflow movements.

Second, with respect to the existence of different tax regulations, tariffs, and duties systems in different foreign countries, tax liability reduction of the new foreign investment projects can be achieved by transferring goods to the foreign subsidiary at the lowest possible transfer prices, if the country has low income tax rates, and by transferring goods out (selling to other subsidiaries) at the highest possible transfer prices. The global tax liability of a MNE will be minimized and overall global profits will be increased as a result of the new foreign investment project.

Third, with respect to the exchange rate risk, transfer pricing policies are considered to be one of the best means to minimize foreign exchange losses from currency fluctuations or to shift the losses from one foreign investment project to another by moving assets from one country to another under the fluctuating exchange rate system. This can be done by determining what currency is to be used for payment. Top management must determine whether the buying or selling foreign investment project or subsidiary has the foreign exchange risk. If this is done, the transfer pricing will have significant effects on the net cash flows of the foreign investment. Therefore, to accept or reject a capital investment project for a MNE, top management must design the appropriate international transfer

Figure 5.1
International Transfer Pricing Policies and Capital
Budgeting Decisions

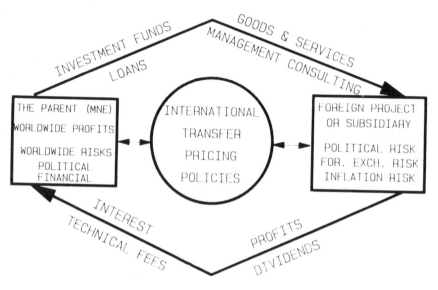

pricing system that will lead to capital budgeting decisions that positively affect the MNE's global profits over the long run.

On the other hand, international transfer pricing policies may result in suboptimal decisions on capital investment projects, but only if they are the only information available and used to make the decisions.[2] However, to evaluate a foreign investment project, using both full-cost and market-based transfer prices may lead to making the right investment decision.[3] Also, Alan Shapiro emphasized that transfer prices may significantly distort the profitability of a capital investment project. He added that a MNE should use the market-based transfer prices to evaluate capital investment project inputs. When the external market does not exist for the intermediate product, the MNE must use the cost savings or the additional revenues or profits generated to the MNE from the foreign investment project to evaluate the project.[4]

The decision process for a capital budgeting project of a MNE can be grouped in four different stages:

1. Identification of international business opportunities in foreign countries that need to be explored and/or problems associated with overseas investments that need to be solved by using capital expenditures

2. Analysis of foreign investment projects in terms of cash inflows and outflows; political, financial, and business risks; and different foreign tax systems and regulations

3. Evaluation and comparison of different international investment projects with other projects and selection of one or more capital projects by using appropriate techniques that are relevant to the complexities of the international business environment

4. Implementation and control of the selected project by comparison of the actual with the expected results to identify causes for any variances, provide subsidiary managers and top management (the decision makers) with information on the total effect of these variances on the MNE as a whole, and suggest a solution (either to continue the investment in the current project or discontinue)

Only the first three steps will be the subject of discussion in detail in the following sections.

The Identification Process

A MNE has a major challenge in doing business abroad. Therefore, it is essential to find and identify successful international investment opportunities to ensure expansion and higher global profitability within the political, economic, and social environmental limitations in the worldwide business, and to identify the need for additional production capacities.

The identification of potential international capital investment projects is a key (starting) process rather than an analysis process.[5] A clearly well-defined investment process will help a MNE to analyze, evaluate, and select the appropriate international investment project that will be in accord with the MNE's global strategies, policies, and goals.

Certain information needs to be collected within the identification process. MNEs need information on demographic changes in foreign countries, domestic and international industry trends, local and international competitors, cultural attitudes toward foreign investments, income taxes imposed on foreign investments, and political factors and their effect on cash flows of foreign investment projects. Most of the information needed for the identification process can be characterized as being external, nonfinancial, and ex ante.[6] In this case, a MNE may face a problem of how to quantify these factors to use them as input in the capital budgeting decision process.

The Analysis of Capital Budgeting Projects

Unlike domestic firms, MNEs face many complicated issues when analyzing different foreign investment projects. These issues include political risks and their effects on cash flows, foreign tax regulations, inflation, blocked funds, expropriations, exchange rate fluctuations, and many other factors associated with international business transactions. To alleviate these problems, a MNE has to analyze the estimated cash inflows and outflows of the foreign project over the expected or selected evaluation period.

The expected cash receipts and disbursements start with the market expectations and are similar to cash operating budgets. The MNE may use the information collected in the identification stage to make its demand forecasts and use these forecasts to arrive at its expected sales over the period of the project. The next step is to predict the expected costs of operating the project or subsidiary and the service fees or charges, which are basically a form of transfer prices, to be remitted to the parent. The analysis of cash flows (including the cost of funding, the cash inflows during the useful life of the investment, and the salvage value of the project) moves from the foreign subsidiary level to the parent level to predict how much cash will be transferred from the subsidiary to the parent, at what time, and in what form.[7]

Restrictions on cash outflow movements imposed by the foreign country and the fluctuations of the exchange rates are major factors in determining the transfer price to be used. MNEs would like to maximize their global net cash flow from projects. Different channels are available for MNEs to (a) reinvest the net cash flows in other existing foreign subsidiaries, (b) pay dividends, (c) pay debt obligations, or (d) reinvest in new projects.[8]

MNEs need to know the restrictions imposed by foreign governments, such as tax regulations, laws, and exchange controls, which may limit any conversion or movement of profits, interests, consulting technical fees, royalties, or dividends from the foreign subsidiary to the parent. Under such circumstances, MNEs must use transfer pricing techniques to alleviate the negative impact of such government restrictions on cash management of the foreign investment projects. However, transfer pricing policies for goods and servies among subsidiaries themselves or with the parent can significantly distort the profitability of a proposed capital investment project.[9] The market price is considered to be the most appropriate price to be used to evaluate cash inflows and outflows of the investment project, and in the case of nonexistence of the intermediate market, global cost savings or incremental profits resulting from the investment project must be used.[10]

Since only after-tax net cash flows are relevant for capital budgeting decisions, the tax structure of the host country is an important issue that needs to be analyzed. The analysis would include the income taxes imposed on income associated with foreign investment projects, indirect taxes, tax treaties, foreign tax credits, and the effective tax rates. The actual taxes to be paid to foreign countries on investment projects are a function of many different factors, and the form of remittance is believed to be among the important ones.[11] The forms of remittance include dividends, royalties, loan payments, interest payments, management consulting technical fees, and transfer price adjustments. To maximize the net realizable cash flows from the project, the transfer prices of technical fees, royalties, and other services such as forms of funds transferred back to the parent should be set as high as possible.[12]

Political risk is one of the most important inputs for capital budgeting decisions. Political risk is defined as the "unanticipated changes in political factors that affect the relative prices of traded factors of production, goods, and services."[13] Political risk may have a significant impact on the net cash flows of foreign investment projects. The greater the extent of control that the most powerful political group of a country exercises over capital investment projects, in terms of cash inflows and outflows, the greater the political risk.[14]

Expropriation of foreign investments by the host government is only one factor of political risk. Other factors include additional taxes on new investments, restrictions on imports of new materials, government intervention in labor and union negotiations, and requirements that new investments be in the form of joint ventures with local firms having the majority of ownership.[15]

Therefore, political risk should be analyzed, measured, and evaluated before making a decision on any capital investment project. Shapiro describes five different alternative methods for incorporating the political risk into the capital budgeting analysis process:[16]

1. Shortening the payback period to the minimum
2. Raising the required rate of return of the investment
3. Adjusting the cash flows for the cost of risk insurance
4. Adjusting of cash flows to reflect the impact of the political risk
5. Using certainty equivalents rather than expected cash flows

Exchange rate fluctuations can have a significant effect on expected cash flows of capital investment projects. They also affect costs and revenues of the project. The expected or anticipated exchange rate of different countries should be included for each project to be considered. Inflation is another factor associated with exchange rate fluctuations.

It is suggested that the projections of all items of capital investment should be made, first, in terms of the local currency to show the effect of the changes in the exchange rates on cost and revenues. Net returns can then be converted into the parent's currency to make all capital projects of different countries comparable from the parent's viewpoint.[17] It is obvious that the effect of both inflation and exchange rate changes makes capital budgeting decisions more complicated for international projects than for domestic ones.

Evaluation and Comparisons of Capital Budgeting Projects

In this stage the alternative capital budgeting projects are evaluated, using appropriate techniques, and then compared with each other and ranked on the basis of the expected net return on initial investment. Once a MNE has analyzed different factors of all possible capital budgeting projects, top management must use an appropriate technique to select one or more projects out of many possible ones. In the following sections, traditional capital budgeting techniques will be discussed first; then the appropriate technique that will incorporate the effects of political risk, inflation, different tax rates of different countries, and foreign exchange rate fluctuations will be considered.

Payback Period

The payback period provides a measure of the time that it will take for a project to generate net cash flows to recover the initial amount invested. The payback period can be computed by dividing the initial cash outflow after taxes (of both host and home countries) for the project by the after-tax cash inflows expected to be received from the foreign project, or it can be calculated as follows:

$$P = \frac{COAT_0}{\sum_{t=1}^{P} CIAT_t}$$

where

$P =$ Payback period

$COAT_0 =$ The initial outlay after tax for the project

$CIAT_t =$ The cash inflows expected to be received after tax (payable to both host and home countries)

$t =$ time period, $t = 1$ is the first year for example.

This technique emphasizes two major issues: the liquidity of the investment project and capital recovery. It ignores the time value of money, the profitability of the project over the longer term, the expected revenues beyond the payback period, and political risks associated with international capital budgeting projects.

For MNEs, the payback period technique can be used as a liquidity constraint rather than as a way for making the choice among capital budgeting projects.[18] Political risks can be incorporated into this simple model by requiring a shorter payback period for investment projects in countries that are more likely to have unstable political conditions. Another way to adjust the payback period model is to charge the annual expected cash inflows after tax a premium for political and economic risk insurance.[19]

The Accounting Rate of Return on Investment (ROI)

There are several variations and results of the accounting rate of return method. A general rule is to divide the average annual net income from the project by the cost of the foreign investment.

Annual net income has been defined in many different ways. It can be net operating income before taxes or after taxes, controllable net operating income by the foreign subsidiary manager, or the total contribution margin of the investment in the project. The cost of the investment may be defined as the gross book value of the asset, the net book value, the current or replacement cost, or the average return based on average expected net income for a number of years.

The accounting rate of return technique, unlike the payback technique, considers profitability as an objective. ROI is supposed to have the following advantages:[20]

1. It is a single comprehensive figure influenced by everything that has happened that affects the financial status of a subsidiary—and that is a lot in the case of a foreign subsidiary.
2. It measures how well the subsidiary manager uses the property of a company to generate profits.
3. Rate of return is a common denominator that can be compared directly among subsidiaries, among subsidiaries and outside companies, or among subsidiaries and alternative investment—a very useful tool in multinational operations.

However, there are many difficulties in using ROI as the companywide criterion for measuring performance in MNEs. First, "ROI oversimplifies a very complex decision making process."[21] ROI can give a picture of managerial performance only if top management intends to measure the utilization of assets controlled by managers rather than the performance of managers themselves. ROI tries to combine three major elements in one single measure—planning, decision making, and control.[22] Using a single rate of return for each foreign investment is too simple to serve as a basis for all trade-offs between investments and profits in a MNE.

Second, with respect to the numerator, the measurement of foreign investment project income for rate of return calculation is complicated by intracompany transactions. The effect of one foreign investment project on the return streams of other subsidiaries needs to be accounted for; however, such assessments are difficult to make.[23]

Third, with respect to the denominator, it is difficult to obtain a satisfactory monetary basis for the value of the investment. For example, using the gross book value of the investment base may lead to suboptimal decisions, because a manager may increase his or her ROI by scrapping perfectly useful assets that do not contribute profits equal to the foreign subsidiary's goal.

Fourth, foreign operations are often established for strategic economic motivations for going abroad rather than for profit maximization. However, top management forgets this fact when evaluating the performance of foreign projects. Therefore, using a companywide performance (ROI) criterion to evaluate the profitability of foreign investments is inadequate and misleading as well.

Fifth, the reported results of any foreign investment or subsidiary are directly affected by many environmental constraints. Social, economic, political, legal, and educational policies and actions of host governments can drastically affect the reported results of a foreign investment. Foreign exchange controls have a significant effect on both an investment's and a manger's performance,[24] and since MNEs conduct business in many countries, top management must decide the extent to which managers of foreign investment projects are to be held responsible for foreign exchange losses.[25]

Net Present Value

The net present value (NPV) is defined as the present value of future cash inflows after taxes to be derived from the foreign investment project, discounted at the required rate of return or cost of capital, minus the initial net cash outlay after tax for the project. Mathematically, the net present value is represented by the following formula:

$$NPV = \left| \frac{CIAT_1}{(1 + K)^1} + \frac{CIAT_2}{(1 + K)^2} + ... + \frac{CIAT_n}{(1 + K)^n} \right| - COAT_0$$

$$= \sum_{i=1}^{n} \frac{CIAT_i}{(1 + K)^i} - CIAT_0$$

where

$CIAT_i$ — Cash inflows after tax derived from the foreign project in period i

$COAT_0$ = Initial after-tax cash investment

K = The appropriate discount rate

n = The investment horizon

If the net present value is positive, the project is desirable because it is expected to yield a return that will exceed the cost of capital; if the NPV is negative, the project is undesirable because the yields are not enough to cover the cost of capital. When there are more than one foreign project, the one with the largest NPV is most desirable. The NPV model has become widely used for the capital budgeting decision-making process because it considers the time value of money and earnings over the life of a project, focuses on cash rather than accounting profits, and emphasizes the opportunity cost of the capital invested.

For MNEs, it is necessary to quantify and incorporate all or most of the factors associated with foreign investments and their complexities into the NPV model. This can be done by adjusting the appropriate discount rate, expected cash flows, or both, or adding another quantitative variable to the model to reflect the impact of environmental variables, such as political risks, foreign exchange risk, the effect of inflation, and the effect of transfer pricing policies.

A normative model for the capital budgeting decisions of foreign projects using the NPV technique is presented here. The model may be considered a comprehensive one since it includes the effects of inflation, political risks (including expropriation), foreign exchange risk, and transfer pricing policies.

The model can be expressed as follows:

$$NPV = \left| \sum_{i=1}^{y-1} \frac{CIAT_i(1 - E_i)}{(1 + K)^i(1 + I_r)^i} + (1 - P_y) \sum^{y} \frac{CIAT_i(1 - E_i)}{(1 + K)^i(1 + I_r)^i} \right.$$

$$\left. + \sum \frac{S(1 + r)_i}{(1 + K)^i} + \sum \frac{TP_i}{(1 + K)^i} \right| - COAT_0$$

where

$CIAT_i$ = Cash inflows after tax from the project in period i

E_i = The expected forward exchange discount in period i

$(1 - E_i)$ = The cost of a foreign exchange risk management

K = The appropriate discount rate

I_r = Inflation rate in a foreign country

$(1 + I_r)^i$ = The premium for the anticipated inflation rate in a foreign country

y = The year when expropriation by a foreign government is expected

P_y = The probability of expropriation in year y, and if there is no expropriation in year y, with probability $(1 - P_y)$ cash inflows from the foreign investment will continue to be generated; however, if expropriation does happen, future cash inflows will be affected negatively in year y and thereafter

$S(1 + r)_n$ = Incremental returns of unremitted profits after tax (host and home countries) that are reinvested to the end of the project's useful life (n) at the local reinvestment rate (r) and discount the salvage value to the present by $1/(1 + K)^i$

TP_i = The incremental revenues or incremental savings resulting from using transfer pricing policies for selling to and buying from the foreign investment project at different prices than arm's-length transactions to achieve certain global goals for the MNE

$COAT_0$ = Initial after-tax cash investment

The NPV model, as suggested earlier, includes the effect of four different factors: (1) foreign exchange rate fluctuations, (2) inflation in a foreign country where the project is expected to be located, (3) transfer pricing policies, and (4) political risks.

The effect of foreign exchange rate fluctuations is incorporated into the NPV model in the term $(1 - E_i)$. The term means that each annual cash inflow generated by a foreign investment is to be charged with a premium for economic risk such as currency fluctuations. In other words, each annual cash inflow needs to be adjusted for the cost of an exchange risk management program.[26] Expected cash inflows need to be adjusted for the effect of inflation in the foreign country by including the premium for the anticipated inflation $(1 - I_r)^i$ in a foreign country.

The political risk has been integrated into the NPV model in two different terms: (1) the effect of expropriation on the foreign investment project as measured by

$$(1 - Py) \sum_{i=1}^{y} \frac{CIAT_i (1 - E_i)}{(1 + K)^i (1 + I_r)^i}$$

and (2) the cost of managing the foreign exchange risk as measured by $(1 - E_i)$ in arriving at the present value of the cash inflows before year y. Political risk is an essential factor to be considered in capital budgeting decisions, especially in the international market, because it is a major input for making the right decision. However, political risk can not be easily predicted, measured, and quantified, because there is a high degree of uncertainty associated with doing business overseas.

Some researchers have tried to measure the political risk within the context of capital budgeting decisions. For example, Tamir Agmon states that a capital budgeting project may be affected by two external political environments, vulnerability and cost, and he believes that political dependence is a function of these two factors. Agmon defines the vulnerability as "the probability that a political event that has an effect on the project will occur."[27] Examples of political risk include imposed public ownership, changes in tax regulations and tax structure, and many other forms of government intervention. Agmon defines the cost of political risk as "the actual impact on the cash flows of a given project if a given political contingency occurs."[28]

Agmon uses a two-by-two matrix that includes high-low vulnerability combined with high-low cost situations, and he believes that firms should be concerned only minimally with high vulnerability, high-cost situations.[29] However, the author believes that Agmon's model is too simple to deal with the very complicated foreign environment and may not be sufficient to lead to the optimal selection of capital budgeting projects.

The effect of the transfer pricing policies, as incorporated into the NPV model, is the present value of the incremental revenues or incremental savings resulting from the use of these policies, which have a significant impact on almost all the components of the NPV model. A transfer pricing policy is an essential factor in determining how much cash or funds can be withdrawn from a foreign investment project through the use of high or low transfer prices for goods, services such as management service fees, or any other transfers such as dividends or royalties.

Another aspect of incremental savings that can be affected by using transfer pricing policies is the reduction of the tax liabilities of the new foreign investment by transferring goods or services to or from other foreign subsidiaries or the parent at low or high transfer prices to minimize the tax liability of foreign investment projects. In this case, the global net tax savings to be generated from any expected business transactions with the proposed foreign investment should be added to the expected cash inflow of the new project, and any artificial profits or losses resulting from the transfer pricing policies should be excluded.

A third aspect of using transfer pricing policies as input for capital budgeting decisions is to minimize the foreign exchange rate risk. When transfer pricing policies are used to minimize losses from the fluctuations of foreign exchange rates or to shift the losses from one foreign investment project to another, it is necessary for the MNE to include the net global effect resulting from the use of such policies as a part of the cash flows of the foreign investment and consequently to integrate this effect into the NPV of the project with which the net savings are associated.

Finally, for capital budgeting decisions, MNEs should design the appropriate international transfer pricing system or policy that will lead them to make optimum capital budgeting decisions by choosing the best alternative that will help them in achieving the global objectives of the MNE in the long run.

SUMMARY AND CONCLUSIONS

Five different types of managerial decisions are most widely used with transfer pricing policies: (*a*) capital investment budgeting decisions, (*b*) the decision of whether to manufacture the product internally or buy it from the external market, (*c*) product pricing decisions for the external customers of both intermediate and final products, (*d*) output-level decisions, and (*e*) MNEs' strategic decisions. Capital budgeting decisions are the only ones discussed in this book.

The first step of a capital budgeting decision process is to find and identify successful international investment opportunities to ensure expansion and higher global profitability within political, economic, and sociological environmental limitations in the worldwide business. The second step is to analyze foreign investment projects in terms of cash inflows and outflows; political, financial, and business risks; and different foreign tax systems and regulations. The third step is to evaluate and compare different international investment projects with each other and select one or more of them by using appropriate techniques that are relevant to the complexities of the international business environment.

Traditional capital budgeting techniques, such as payback period, the accounting rate of return on investment (ROI), and the net present value (NPV) approach are discussed first; then a modified and comprehensive NPV technique is suggested. The suggested technique includes the effect of four different factors: (1) foreign exchange rate fluctuations, (2) inflation in a foreign country where the project is expected to be located, (3) transfer pricing policies, and (4) the effect of political risks.

NOTES

1. Robert G. Eccles, *The Transfer Pricing Problem: A Theory for Practice* (Lexington, Mass.: Lexington Books, 1985), 10–11.

2. Ibid., 68.

3. Ibid.

4. Alan Shapiro, *Multinational Financial Management*, (Boston: Allyn and Bacon, 1986), 433.

5. Lawrence A. Gordon and George E. Pinches, *Improving Capital Budgeting: A Decision Support System Approach* (Reading, Mass.: Addison-Wesley Publishing Company, 1984), 36.

6. Ibid., 37.

7. Stefan H. Robock and Kenneth Simmonds, *International Business and Mutinational Enterprises*, 3rd ed. (Homewood, Ill.: Richard D. Irwin, 1983), 519.

8. John J. Clark, Thomas J. Hindelang, and Robert E. Pritchard, *Capital Budgeting: Planning and Control of Capital Expenditures*, 2nd ed. (Englewood Cliffs, N.J.: Prentice-Hall, 1984), 422.

9. Shapiro, *Multinational Financial Management,* 432.

10. Ibid., 433.

11. Ibid., 437.

12. Ibid.

13. Tamir Agmon, *Political Economy and Risk in World Financial Markets* (Lexington, Mass.: Lexington Books, 1985), 2.

14. Ibid., 56.

15. Joseph A. Maciariello, *Management Control Systems* (Englewood Cliffs, N.J.: Prentice-Hall, 1984), 562.

16. Shapiro, *Multinational Financial Management*, 438–40.

17. Maciariello, *Management Control Systems*, 565.

18. Clark, Hindelang, and Pritchard, *Capital Budgeting*, 32.

19. Arthur Stonehill and Leonard Nathanson, "Capital Budgeting and the Multinational Corporation," *California Management Review* (Summer 1968): 39–54, as quoted in Shapiro, *Multinational Financial Management*, 439.

20. Edward C. Bursk, John Dearden, David F. Hawkins, and Victor M. Longstreet, *Financial Control of Multinational Operations* (New York: Financial Executives Research Foundation, 1971), 17-18.

21. Harold Bierman, "ROI as a Measure of Managerial Performance," in *Accounting for Managerial Decision Making*, ed. Don T. Decoster et al., 2nd ed. (Santa Barbara, Calif.: Wiley/Hamilton, 1978), 403.

22. Ibid., 410.

23. Fredrick D. S. Choi and Gerhard G. Mueller, *An Introduction to Multinational Accounting*, (Englewood Cliffs, N.J.: Prentice-Hall, 1978), 267.

24. William Persen and Van Lessig, *Evaluating the Financial Performance of Overseas Operations* (New York: Financial Executives Research Foundation, 1978), 45.

25. Sidney M. Robbins and Robert B. Stobaugh, "The Bent Measuring Stick for Foreign Subsidiaries," *Harvard Business Review* (January–February 1977): 35.

26. Shapiro, *Multinational Financial Management*, 439.

27. Agmon. *Political Economy and Risk*, 59.

28. Ibid., 60.

29. Ibid., 60-61.

6

International Transfer Pricing Policies and Taxation

For the past two decades, MNEs have had no business function that goes as deeply into nearly all international operations, including manufacturing, marketing, management, and financing, as transfer pricing. International transfer pricing decisions have great impact on the international operations of MNEs, directly affecting their global revenues and profits, and can help or limit a MNE's ability to operate, manage, and utilize its economic resources on a global basis for the purpose of achieving its ultimate goals.

Tax regulations of the United States are different from those of foreign countries in many aspects, such as tax rates, tax treaties, tax bases, foreign tax credits, and taxes imposed on any profits resulting from using intracompany transfer pricing policies for goods and services crossing the border of the country. Among foreign countries there are great differences in many aspect in their tax regulations and laws. Developed countries, such as the United Kingdom, Canada, Sweden, France, Japan, and Switzerland, have different objectives in their tax structures, policies, and regulations than do less developed countries, such as Chile, Mexico, Zaire, Saudi Arabia, Bahrain, and Korea, among others.

Developed countries impose taxes on their multinational and foreign corporations for four main purposes:

1. To raise revenues
2. To provide tax incentives
3. To avoid or minimize double taxation
4. To curb tax abuses

Less developed countries (LDC) use their tax systems to some extent, for different objectives:

1. To achieve certain rates of economic growth
2. To establish industrial priorities
3. To encourage new investments in new industries
4. To maintain political and social stability by sustained development of the economy
5. To monitor all foreign exchange transactions and enforce stringent control

However, some less developed countries relax their governmental restrictions on the repatriation or remittance of profits, capital, or income of foreign investments to encourage more inward investment in their countries.

Over the long run, different tax structures, different tax rates of foreign countries on foreign investments and subsidiaries, and different foreign exchange control policies may constitute the most basic reason for using the right strategy for international transfer pricing policies combined with long-range global tax planning to achieve the global objectives of MNEs within the different environmental conditions in the worldwide market. This chapter will discuss two major issues: (1) Section 482 of the U.S. Internal Revenue Code and its impact on the international activities of MNEs, and (2) the tax systems of selected foreign countries and their impact on MNEs in using international transfer pricing policies.

UNITED STATES TAXATION OF INTERNATIONAL TRANSFER TRANSACTIONS

International transfer pricing decisions have significant impact on global sales, tax liabilities, and profits of MNEs. Tax authorities of most countries throughout the world require that the transfer pricing policies between related entitites be at arm's length. Their objectives are (*a*) to prevent MNEs from reducing their tax liabilities by shifting profits from one entity to another, (*b*) to allow tax authorities to adjust income and deductions to reflect clearly the correct taxable income within their territories, and (*c*) to counter abusive transfer pricing policies. Most legislation of different countries has focused on the concept of comparing intracompany prices with arm's-length third-party prices.

In the United States, Section 482 of the U.S. Internal Revenue Code (see Appendix A) provides that the Internal Revenue Service (IRS) may allocate gross income, deductions, credits, or allowances among related entities to prevent the evasion of taxes and to reflect clearly the income of each entity of a corporate group. Related entities under Section 482 are defined as two or more trades, organizations, or businesses owned or controlled, either directly or indirectly, by the same group or interests. The purpose of Section 482 is to prevent shifting of income or profits from one commonly controlled entity to another by a MNE.

Section 482 deals with five types of transactions:

1. Interest charged on intercompany loans
2. Services performed for a related party
3. Use of tangible property by a related party
4. Intercompany transfers of intangible property
5. Intercompany sales of tangible property

Intercompany pricing on sales of tangible property is the most widely known problem; therefore, it will be the one that will be discussed the most in this book.

The application of Section 482 of the U.S. Internal Revenue Code of 1986 has tended to focus on the concept of comparing intragroup transfer prices with arm's-length third-party prices. The arm's length standard is defined by the code as "the amount which would have been charged in independent transactions with unrelated parties under the same or similar circumstances." In other words, Section 482 insists that intracompany transactions be priced at arm's length, or as if they involved unrelated parties in the open market.

Many problems may arise in translating Section 482 into practice by MNEs because the regulations are ambiguous and vague. Consequently, facts and circumstances of what constitutes the appropriate arm's-length price to be used among related entities can give plenty of scope for debate and negotiations. Therefore, most of the disputes between the IRS and MNEs require the courts to settle cases, and there is not one general rule arrived at among courts. A research study by Jane D. Burns concluded that 53% of the sample group of MNEs had Section 482 reallocations in at least one year, and the average annual deficiency proposed by the IRS was about one million dollars, of which 70% was agreed to and paid, 16% was reduced, and 14% was being disputed.[1]

Section 482 prescribed three specific methods for determining arm's-length prices, to be used in order, and a fourth method that may be used for all other situations in which none of the first three is considered appropriate and reasonable. The three methods set forth in the regulations, to be used in order, are (a) comparable uncontrolled price method, (b) resale price method, and (c) cost-plus method. The IRS, in allocating profits or income, should look first for an uncontrolled transaction, second for a resale price, and third at cost of a tangible property plus a reasonable profit. Only if none of these three methods apply is a fourth method used. This method was included in the regulations after vigorous objections by businessmen when the original regulations were issued with only the first three methods. It allows MNEs to use an alternative method to the three methods if they can fully justify the appropriateness and reasonableness of the method selected for their circumstances.[2] In allocating the income or profits of foreign subsidiaries, MNEs have the responsibility for justifying their international transfer pricing methods and proving that they are reasonable. Otherwise, income reallocations made by the IRS must be accepted by the courts unless the MNE proves them to be unreasonable or arbitrary allocations.[3]

Generally, it is not necessary for a MNE to use only one pricing method for all of its products under all circumstances. It may be acceptable for a MNE to sell different products at different stages of completion in different markets using different pricing methods.

Comparable Uncontrolled Price Method

An uncontrolled sale is defined in the regulations as a sale in which the seller and buyer are not members of the same controlled group. In other words, it uses the price charged in comparable sales to third unrelated parties as the appropriate price for intracompany transactions.

Uncontrolled sales can be comparable if the conditions surrounding the sale are either identical to the controlled sales or so nearly identical that differences can be reflected by adjustments to the price. Adjustments are to be made when they reflect differences that have a definitive and reasonable effect on price. The uncontrolled sale, as adjusted, makes up the comparable uncontrolled sale price.

A comparision with sales to third parties is deemed the most appropriate method. However, a major problem, which opens the door for disputes, is how a MNE can validly prove a comparable uncontrolled price. Factors in doing so would include the terms of sale, the timing of sale, the conditions prevailing in the marketplace, transportation costs, and different qualities of products.[4] Generally, the most important issue under this method is whether the sale is truly comparable.

Several problems are encountered in applying the comparable uncontrolled price method in practice.[5] One of the most serious is the absence of unrelated transactions in some industries such as the petroleum industry, where there is vertical integration of global operations handling exploration, production, refining, and shipping. It is seldom practical to find unrelated parties to handle some of the major transactions. Another is that intracompany transfers of intangible property do not fit into the arm's-length standard as required by the regulations. It is difficult, if not impossible, for a firm to sell its valuable advanced technology, marketing know-how, or any intangible assets such as patents to both its own foreign subsidiaries and to unrelated parties who may be its own competitors.

Resale Price Method

If an arm's-length price cannot be determined through the use of a comparable uncontrolled price, the regulations specify that the resale price method must be used. Arm's-length price is computed by looking at a sale by a related buyer to its customers, reduced by an appropriate markup percentage.

The resale price method is appropriate where a sale transaction is made to a controlled party that then resells to an unrelated party and there is no comparable uncontrolled price. A portion of the resale price may be attributable to value added by the related party. In that case, adjustments are to be made to the resale price.

Different guidelines as to the appropriateness of any markup may be used. However, the appropriate markup percentage can be determined from uncontrolled sales made by other resellers under similar circumstances. Generally, there are two methods to compute the markup percentage: the gross profit percentage and the net profit percentage. The regulations prescribe the gross profit percentage method to be used in allocating the income of subsidiaries. However, the net profit percentage can be used as the fourth method.

Cost-Plus Method

The seller's price is computed by multiplying the cost of production by an appropriate gross profit percentage to cover the functions it carries out. The appropriate gross profit percentage can be determined from comparable uncontrolled sales of the seller, another party of the uncontrolled sale, or unrelated parties. This method is usually used by MNEs with major activities in exports of manufacturing components or unfinished goods that have substantial values added to them by the purchasing foreign subsidiaries.

However, the term "cost of production" as prescribed in the regulations should be consistent with sound accounting practices for allocating costs. According to the regulations, if the seller uses its full costs to compute its gross profit percentage, then the cost of production will be the full production costs. If the seller uses direct costs to compute its gross profit percentage, the cost of production will be equal to the direct costs.

The manner in which direct costs are computed may be inconsistent with the regulations' definition of cost of production. In management (or cost) accounting practices, direct costs are defined as those costs that can be traceable to and identified specifically with a particular product or process for a particular purpose. However, direct costing, sometimes called variable costing, is a method of product costing that charges only the variable costs of manufacturing to the product. Variable manufacturing costs include direct materials, direct labor, and variable manufacturing overhead.

Section 482 is not specific about what it means by direct costs. Does it mean the term "direct costs" that includes direct materials and direct labor costs only, or does it mean the product costing method called "direct costing"? The difference between the two is variable manufacturing overhead, which may be between 10% and 30% of production costs.

The Alternative Method

The regulations provide that when none of the three methods can reasonably be applied under the usual circumstances of a particular case, an alternative method should be used. The alternative method can be a variation of one of the three, or an entirely different method that may be appropriate under certain circumstances.

For many years Section 482 has been used as the standard tax treatment of intracompany transfers. It was first adopted in the Revenue Act of 1921 and has remained essentially unchanged since then. A few clarifications and some additional authorities have been given to the IRS over more than 65 years of statutory history.

Today U.S.-based and non-U.S. corporations and their international activities have expanded from only imports and exports to more and more direct involvement in different international markets in many different ways. The growth of U.S.-based and foreign MNEs has brought significant changes in the structure of international markets and has created significant economic interdependence between most nations.[6]

The U.S. Tax Reform Act of 1986 reduced the U.S. corporate tax rates from 40% to 34% on domestic corporations and branches of foreign corporations. The act significantly affects international operations of U.S.-based MNEs and U.S. taxation of foreign MNEs that have subsidiaries in the United States. While the act changed the corporate tax rates, it also made international transfer pricing policies more complicated than before. The majority of accounting practitioners and MNEs' key top executives believed that lowering the U.S. corporate tax rates below those of other industrial developed and developing countries would encourage the US-based MNEs to minimize their global tax liability and consequently maximize their global profits. This could be done by bringing more and more of their taxable income to the United States. However, Section 482 still insists on the use of arm's-length pricing for intercompany transactions.

When MNEs do not deal with their foreign subsidiaries as if they were unrelated, proving the reasonableness of their international transfer pricing in dealing with the IRS may be nearly impossible, especially if their production and marketing techniques are not comparable with any other techniques throughout the world. Another aspect of the U.S. Tax Reform Act of 1986 that creates a potential problem with the transfer price for goods imported into the United States is that a U.S. importer may not claim a transfer price for income tax purposes on goods purchased from a related party that is higher than was claimed for U.S. customs purposes. This restriction prevents companies from reporting a lower transfer price for customs purposes than was reported for income tax purposes and consequently paying lower customs duties. On the other hand, the higher the cost of goods sold used for transfer pricing, the lower the U.S. taxable income that would be used as a basis for income tax liability.

It may be concluded from this analysis that as long as the tax rate differentials are higher than the net effect of tariff rates imposed by the country with the higher tax rate, the higher transfer price will always generate net savings for the MNE. However, if the top management increases the price for goods transferred from one subsidiary to another by a specified amount of money, the higher transfer price may have a negative effect on both the global profits of the MNE and the net income of the buying subsidiary. Generally, the higher the import tariffs relative to the difference in net income tax rates between different countries, the more likely that a lower transfer price is preferable.

THE TAX SYSTEMS OF SELECTED FOREIGN COUNTRIES AND THEIR IMPACT ON INTERNATIONAL TRANSFER PRICING POLICIES

MNEs are the target of tax authorities of all governments all over the world. Most MNEs are based in the highly industrialized and developed countries such as the United States, the United Kingdom, Japan, West Germany, and Canada.

In Canada the federal government imposes a 46% tax rate on Canadian-based MNEs. Canadian-controlled private companies may be granted federal tax reduction. Canadian subsidiaries or branches of foreign MNEs are taxed equally with the Canadian domestic corporations.

In the United Kingdom, all U.K.-based MNEs are liable for a tax rate of 35% on their worldwide profits. A foreign tax credit is allowed for foreign income taxes paid on foreign income taxable in the United Kingdom, with the U.K. tax actually charged on that foreign income as a maximum. Branches of non-U.K. MNEs are liable for income tax at a rate of 35%, the same as the domestic rates, on the British-source income.

In West Germany the profits of German-based MNEs are taxed at the rate of 56% for the undistributed profits and 36% for the distributed earnings. Branches of foreign operations or nonresident corporations are taxed on their profits at the flat tax rate of 50%. This difference in tax rates encourages German corporations to think about making decisions as to whether business operations in Germany should be done through a branch of non-German MNEs, because the 50% rate of corporate tax for foreign subsidiaries or branches in Germany is lower than the tax rate for retained profits of a German corporation.

Japan requires its MNEs to aggregate the loss or income of foreign branches with income or loss of the corporation and pay the Japanese corporate income tax of 33.3% on distributed income or 43.3% on undistributed income on their worldwide income. Branches of foreign MNEs are only taxed on the Japanese-source income in the same manner as the Japanese corporations.

For MNEs, goods and services transferred between two different countries may be priced at two different prices using two different approaches by two different tax authorities for the same item. In addition, different objectives and policies of the tax regulations of the two countries could lead to completely conflicting results. When both tax authorities of the two countries adjust the appropriate transfer price according to their belief about what is called the appropriate arm's-length price, a MNE may be liable for more than a double tax on the same item. Tax treaties among different countries, especially developed countries such as the United States, the United Kingdom, and West Germany, may alleviate the problem. Table 6.1 shows the withholding tax rates under income tax treaties of four different countries: the United States, Canada, the United Kingdom, and West Germany.

Tax treaties are similar to foreign tax credits. By using tax treaties, revenue authorities of different countries try to minimize the impact of double taxation, to encourage cooperation between the revenue authorities, and to exchange information between these authorities. However, tax treaties are applied only to dividends, interest, rent, or royalties. Business profits, which do not include these four items, are taxable at corporate tax rates applicable in the host country to business profits in general. Tax treaties do not eliminate double taxation completely, in most cases; they only reduce the tax rate on income. Dividends, for example, are taxed by both host and home countries, who are parties to tax treaties, but at different lower rates.

Despite the tax treaties among countries, MNEs are still required to pay high income tax liabilities over their global profits as a cost of

Table 6.1
Withholding Tax Rates under Income Tax Treaties

	UNITED STATES	CANADA	UNITED KINGDOM	WEST GERMANY
UNITED STATES				
DIVIDENDS	--	15%	15%	15%
INTEREST	--	15%	EXEMPT	EXEMPT
PATENT KNOW-HOW				
ROYALTIES	--	10%	EXEMPT	EXEMPT
CANADA				
DIVIDENDS	15%	--	15%	15%
INTEREST	15%	--	10%	15%
PATENT KNOW HOW				
ROYALTIES	10%	--	10%	15%
UNITED KINGDOM				
DIVIDENDS	15%	15%	--	15%
INTEREST	EXEMPT	10%	--	EXEMPT
PATENT KNOW-HOW				
ROYALTIES	EXEMPT	10%	--	EXEMPT
WEST GERMANY				
DIVIDENDS	15%	15%	15%	--
INTEREST	EXEMPT	15%	EXEMPT	--
PATENT KNOW-HOW				
ROYALTIES	EXEMPT	15%	EXEMPT	--

doing business across the border. Every revenue authority tries to come up with the arm's-length price, which may not be in existence in reality when the product is unique in the international market. In the following sections we will discuss each country separately in terms of the effect of the tax system on international intracompany transfer pricing policies.

Canada

The Department of National Revenue Canada has issued Section 69 of the Income Tax Act, which applies to intracompany transactions. Section 69(2) provides that the amount that the taxpayer in Canada has paid or agreed to pay to the nonresident may not, for tax purposes, exceed a reasonable arm's-length price. On the other hand, the amount a nonresident not dealing at arm's-length has paid or agreed to pay to a Canadian taxpayer may not, for tax purposes, be less than a reasonable arms'-length price. The reasonable arm's-length price is described in Section 69 as the amount that would have been reasonable in the circumstances if the parties to the transaction had been dealing at arm's length, and may mean fair market value or another amount depending on the circumstances surrounding each case.

In February 1987 Revenue Canada published official guidelines on transfer pricing through Circular 87-2. The guidelines give detailed descriptions of Revenue Canada's approach in interpreting the broadly worded statutory provisions. Under the arm's-length principle, each transaction between two related parties should be carried out under the terms and at a price that one could reasonably have expected in similar circumstances had the parties been dealing at arm's length. In applying the arm's-length principle, the department follows the 1979 Organization for Economic Cooperation and Development (OECD) report *Transfer Pricing and Multinational Enterprises*, which reflects international practices in most developed and developing countries.

The Canadian taxes on intracompany transactions are very similar to those of the United States and the OECD. The three methods set forth in Revenue Canada's Transfer Pricing Circular are (1) the comparable uncontrolled price, (2) cost-plus, and (3) resale price. Other methods may also be used in support of one of these three methods or in circumstances where none of the three methods is appropriate.

The United Kingdom

In 1970 the Inland Revenue included Section 485 in the Tax Act, to deal with the international transfer pricing of intracompany transactions between a company resident in the United Kingdom and an overseas affiliate. The objective of Section 485 is to prevent using artificial intracompany transfer pricing policies to move profits from the United Kingdom to other countries. Section 485 is also used to ensure that all goods sold to or purchased from overseas affiliates are not sold at an understated value or purchased at an overstated value.

Under Section 485, the Inland Revenue can adjust the taxable income of the U.K. business entity in any transfer transaction with an overseas affiliate to clearly reflect the amount that would have resulted if the prices used had been those that would have applied between two unrelated parties, which is the arm's-length price. Section 485 is used when one of the parties to a transfer transaction controls the other party or both are under the control of a third party.

To decide the appropriate transfer price, it would be necessary to investigate the pricing structure and policies of an independent business entity that has similar assets and liabilities, has identical products with the same product mix and market share, is working in the same geographical territories, and has the same organizational structure. The difficulty or impossibility of proving this is very obvious, especially when the transfer transactions involve unique assets or circumstances where no identical arm's-length price exists.

The U.K. Inland Revenue authorities have not issued any guidelines on intercompany transfer pricing. However, a report was issued by the OECD in 1979 on *Transfer Pricing and Multinational Enterprises*. This report may be used in the United Kingdom because it represents generally agreed practices in the United States, Canada, Japan, Italy, New Zealand, and Sweden, among others.[7] The OECD report attempts to set out as far as possible the considerations to be taken into account in determining international transfer prices for tax purposes. The Inland Revenue participated in the preparation of the OECD report. Therefore, it is an acceptable guideline for setting the transfer pricing policies for corporations doing business in the United Kingdom. In 1981 the Research and Technical Committee of the Institute of Cost and Management Accountants (ICMA, London) whose name has since changed to the Chartered Institute of Management Accounts (CIMA), issued management accounting guidelines on interunit transfer pricing (see Appendix B) based on the practice of British business firms.

West Germany

Under German tax law, a taxpayer's income may be adjusted upward to reflect what should have been an arm's-length price if its international business transactions reduced the taxable income as a result of business dealings at a price less than an appropriate arm's-length price. In February 1983 German authorities issued detailed regulations on the intracompany transfer pricing issue. Although they have helped taxpayers in dealing with some issues, they have created problems for MNEs due to their rigidity.[8] The German tax authorities may require from MNEs detailed documentation for the justification of using their international transfer pricing policies.

Arm's-length price is required to be determined for two reasons: (1) to establish whether the terms and conditions that have been agreed on differ from the arm's-length price, and (2) to determine the extent of the reallocation based on the established arm's-length transfer price as determined in (1).[9] However, there are no specific criteria to be used to determine the appropriate arm's-length price. Therefore, the criteria used by the tax administration are similar to those of Section 482 of the U.S. Internal Revenue Code.[10]

Japan

Prior to November 1980 the Japanese government had used both the Foreign Investment Law and the Foreign Exchange and Trade Law to control foreign investment. All these restrictions were necessary after World War II because of the poor foreign currency situation. In the 1950s the government started to encourage the inflow of foreign capital in certain areas. In 1964 Japan joined the OECD and has become a free trade country.

In 1980 the Foreign Investment Law was eliminated, and the Foreign Exchange and Trade Control Law was amended to include all matters related to foreign investment and operations. In 1986 Japan issued new legislation dealing with intracompany transfer pricing rules, to be effective from April 1, 1986. It is considered to be the first comprehensive set of rules to counter tax avoidance by the use of artifical international transfer pricing policies. The law requires that intracompany cross-border transactions be consummated at the same prices as would be determined between unrelated parties, that is, the arm's-length price. The arm's-length price should be determined by applying any one of the following methods:

1. Third party comparable price
2. Resale price
3. Cost-plus
4. Others

Any of the first three methods can be used. However, the fourth method may be used only if the first three methods are not applicable. The law provides specific guidance on the rules to be used. These rules are similar to those adopted by Section 482 of the U.S. Internal Revenue Code and outlined in the 1979 OECD report.

THE ORGANIZATION FOR ECONOMIC COOPERATION AND DEVELOPMENT REPORT ON INTRACOMPANY TRANSFER PRICING

In May 1979 the Council of the Organization for Economic Cooperation and Development (OECD) issued a report on intracompany transfer pricing prepared by the OECD Committee on Fiscal Affairs and adopted the recommendation included in the report. The report, *Transfer Pricing and Multinational Enterprises*, includes two major issues on intracompany transfer pricing: (1) considerations to be taken into account in determining the appropriate international transfer prices for tax purposes, and (2) description of the generally agreed practices of transfer pricing policies in developed countries for tax purposes. The report concentrates on the major problems of determining transfer prices. However, it does not discuss specific cases or circumstances that can be applicable to a specific country, a specific industry, a specific MNE, or a specific geographical area.

The OECD report has significantly affected the views and attitudes of revenue authorities throughout the world. The report is very similar to Section 482 of the U.S. Internal Revenue Code. The U.K. revenue authorities participated in the preparation of the report. Canada, Japan, and West Germany, among other members of the committee, have very similar tax laws, tax regulations, and guidelines to those adopted by the United States and outlined in the 1979 OECD report on transfer pricing.

While the 1979 OECD report has no binding authority in the OECD member countries, it does provide an indication of the rules and approaches adopted by one revenue authority in a country with a well-developed tax system, the United States. The acceptance of the 1979 OECD report on transfer pricing by the Business and Industry Committee, representing business interests in major countries, is evidence that there is significant support for worldwide adoption of the U.S. tax rules on transfer pricing.[11]

SUMMARY

The major issues are discussed in this chapter: (1) Section 482 of the U.S. Internal Revenue Code and its impact on the international activities of MNEs, and (2) the tax systems of selected foreign countries and their impact on MNEs in using ITP policies. Section 482 prescribes three specific methods for determining arm's-length prices, to be used in order, and a fourth method that may be used for all other situations in which none of the first three is considered appropriate and reasonable. The three methods set forth in the regulations are (a) comparable uncontrolled price, (b) resale price, and (c) cost-plus. Only if none of these three methods apply, is a fourth method used. This allows MNEs to use an alternative method if they can fully justify the appropriateness and reasonableness of the method selected for their circumstances.

Under the U.S. Tax Reform Act of 1986, lowering the U.S. corporate tax rates below those of other industrial developed and developing countries may encourage the U.S.-based MNEs to minimize their global tax liabilities and consequently increase their global profits. This could be done by bringing more of their taxable income to the United States. However, there are many problems associated with the IRS insistence on the use of arm's-length pricing for intracompany transactions.

The transfer of goods and services between two different countries may be priced at two different prices using two different approaches by the two different tax authorities for the same item. Also, different objectives and policies of tax regulations of different countries could lead to conflicting results. When different tax authorities of two countries adjust the appropriate transfer price according to their belief on what is called the appropriate arm's-length price, a MNE may be liable for more than a double tax liability on the same item.

NOTES

1. Jane O. Burns, "How IRS Applies the Intercompany Pricing Rules of Section 482: A Corporate Survey," *Journal of Taxation* (May 1980): 308–14.

2. Business International Corporation, *Setting Intercorporate Pricing Policies*, Business International Research Report (New York: Business International Corporation 1973), 39–40.

3. Jane O. Burns, "The Multinational Enterprise: U.S. Taxation of Foreign Source Income," in *International Acccounting*, ed. H. Peter Holzer and others (New York: Harper and Row Publishers, 1984), 140.

4. Howard M. Liebman, "International Transfer Pricing and Recent Development: Part I," *Tax Planning International Review* (August 1987): 4.

5. Guenter Schindler, "Intercompany Transfer Pricing after Tax Reform of 1986," *Tax Planning International Review* (November 1987): 9–10.

6. Schindler, "Intercompany Transfer Pricing," 9.

7. Organization for Economic Cooperation and Development, Committee on Fiscal Affairs, *Transfer Pricing and Multinational Enterprises* (Paris Organization for Economic Cooperation and Development, 1979).

8. Terry Symons and Richard Harris, "International Transfer Pricing: Revenue Authorities Put Multinational Business on the Alert," *Tax Planning International Review* (December 1987): 10.

9. Juergen Killius, "Foreign Income Business Operations in West Germany," *Tax Management* (1985): A-61.

10. Ibid., A-62.

11. Dag Helmers, "BOAC's Response to the OECD Report on Transfer Pricing and Multinational Enterprises," *Intertax* (August 1980): 286–93. In Burns, "The Multinational Enterprises: U.S. Taxation of Foreign Source Income," 141.

7

Environmental Factors and Their Effects on Transfer Pricing Decisions

Earlier chapters have dealt with the objectives, techniques, and design of international transfer pricing policies as well as the effect of management decisions on transfer pricing policies. In Chapter 6 we discussed tax systems and tax structures of different countries and their effect on transfer pricing policies. Chapter 6 also covered Section 482 of the U.S. Internal Revenue Code and its impact on the international activities of MNEs. In this chapter, three major groups of environmental factors in the international markets are discussed: economic, sociological, and political-legal factors.

ECONOMIC ENVIRONMENTAL FACTORS

MNEs invest in foreign countries to take advantage of economic differences, such as taxation differences, financial market differences, differences in product costs, and differences in product selling prices in different international markets. The main strategy of MNEs is to produce in the countries where production costs least and sell in the countries where selling prices are highest.[1]

MNEs may sometimes utilize resources more effectively than domestic enterprises by transferring idle or underutilized resources. They also try to use the most efficient and profitable technology in extracting, refining, or manufacturing raw materials in foreign countries.

Inflations, tariff barriers, fluctuating exchange rates, trade barriers and restrictions, balance of payments disequilibriums, and restrictions of foreign trade policies are the most significant economic factors affecting transfer pricing decisions.

Inflation

Inflation is the decline in the general purchasing power of the monetary unit. Wide variations and rapid changes in inflation rates from one country to another are an important factor when MNEs are designing their international transfer pricing policies. In the absence of inflation, transfer pricing policies can be based on costs or cost-plus with confidence in accounting information. However, when prices change, this confidence in accounting information is weakened. Subsidiary managers also find historical cost accounting data inadequate for many managerial decisions.

Higher inflation rates in one country cause prices of goods transferred to another country where lower inflation rates exist to rise, and subsidiaries in the latter country become less competitive. The subsidiary managers in that country find it more difficult to sell their products in the local market, and consequently their competitive position is impaired. Generally, relative inflation rates have an impact on the international business of MNEs.

There is a direct relationship between inflation rates and interest rates. When a country has a lower interest rate, it has a lower inflation rate too than other countries, and vice versa. However, a high inflation rate combined with a higher interest rate in a country may discourage any new investment by MNEs and, consequently, affect the goods transferred to that country.

To illustrate the inflation effect on international transfer pricing policies, let us assume that the inflation rates in countries A and B are 10% and 5% respectively, and the foreign subsidiary A would like to transfer all of its production to another subsidiary domiciled in country B. The global profits of a MNE may be lowered as a result of the higher inflation rate in country A.

As can be seen from Table 7.1, the transfer price, when both countries have the same low inflation rates of 5% is $5.00 per unit of the product transferred. However, when the inflation rate in country A goes up to 10%, the costs of subsidiary A also go up by 10%, and the transfer price increases from $5.00 to $6.00 per unit.

Table 7.1

The Inflation Effect of using High versus Low International Transfer Prices (Higher Inflation Rate in the Seller's Country)

	A	B	THE GLOBE
LOW TRANSFER PRICE & LOW INFLATION RATES			
INFLATION RATE OF COUNTRY A IS 5%			
INFLATION RATE OF COUNTRY B IS 5%			
SALES			
16,000 @ $5.00	$80,000		
16,000 @ $12.00		$192,000	$192,000
LESS: COST OF G.S.	(68,000)	(80,000)	(68,000)
GROSS PROFIT	12,000	112,000	124,000
LESS: S, A, & G EXP.	(10,300)	(75,000)	(85,300)
NET INCOME BEFORE TAX	1,700	37,000	38,700
LESS: INCOME TAX (40%)	(680)	(14,800)	(15,480)
NET INCOME	1,020	22,200	23,220
HIGH TRANSFER PRICE & HIGH INFLATION RATES			
INFLATION RATE OF COUNTRY A IS 10%			
INFLATION RATE OF COUNTRY B IS 5%			
SALES			
16,000 @ $6.00	$ 96,000		
16,000 @ $12.00		$192,000	$192,000
LESS: COST OF G. S.	(71,400)	(96,000)	(71,400)
GROSS PROFIT	24,600	96,000	120,600
LESS: S, A, & G EXP.	(10,815)	(75,000)	(85,815)
NET INCOME BEFORE TAX	13,785	21,000	34,785
LESS: INCOME TAX 40%	(5,514)	(8,400)	(13,914)
NET INCOME	8,271	12,600	20,871

As a result of using different transfer prices in response to the higher inflation rate in country A, the net incomes of both foreign subsidiaries and the MNE as a whole are significantly affected. The global profits of the MNE decrease by more than 10%, from $23,220 to $20,871, as a result of the higher inflation rate of country A. The increase in the transfer price from $5.00 to $6.00 is not enough to cover the increase in the cost of goods sold and operating expenses resulting from a higher inflation rate. Under the high transfer pricing policy, subsidiary A's net income increases from $1,020 to $8,271, while B's net income decreases by more than 43%, from $22,200 to $12,600.

If the difference in inflation rates is in the opposite direction, that is, if country A has the same inflation rate of 5%, but country B has a higher inflation rate of 10%, the effect on the global profits is almost the same as in the previous situation, using the high transfer price at $6.00, as can be seen from Table 7.2. However, subsidiary A would show much higher profits than before, even higher than those of subsidiary B. Subsidiary A's results of operations show a net income of $10,620, more than ten times its net income with a 5% inflation rate, while subsidiary B's operating results show a net income of $10,350, less than 50% of the previous net income reported with a 5% inflation rate.

Table 7.2
The Inflation Effect of using High versus Low International Transfer Prices (Higher Inflation Rate in the Buyer's Country)

	A	B	THE GLOBE
LOW TRANSFER PRICE & LOW INFLATION RATES			
INFLATION RATE OF COUNTRY A IS 5%			
INFLATION RATE OF COUNTRY B IS 5%			
SALES			
16,000 @ $5.00	$80,000		
16,000 @ $12.00		$192,000	$192,000
LESS: COST OF G.S.	(68,000)	(80,000)	(68,000)
GROSS PROFIT	12,000	112,000	124,000
LESS: S, A, & G EXP.	(10,300)	(75,000)	(75,000)
NET INCOME BEFORE TAX	1,700	37,000	38,700
LESS: INCOME TAX (40%)	(680)	(14,800)	(15,480)
NET INCOME	1,020	22,200	23,220
HIGH TRANSFER PRICE & HIGH INFLATION RATES			
INFLATION RATE OF COUNTRY A IS 5%			
INFLATION RATE OF COUNTRY B IS 10%			
SALES			
16,000 @ $6.00	$96,000		
16,000 @ $12.00		$192,000	$192,000
LESS: COST OF G. S.	(68,000)	(96,000)	(68,000)
GROSS PROFIT	28,000	96,000	124,000
LESS: S, A, & G EXP.	(10,300)	(78,750)	(89,050)
NET INCOME BEFORE TAX	17,700	17,250	34,950
LESS: INCOME TAX (40%)	(7,080)	(6,900)	(13,980)
NET INCOME	10,620	10,350	20,970

Tariffs and Duties

Tariffs and duties are another environmental factor that may affect international business activities in general, and especially transfer pricing policies of MNEs. A tariff is the tool most commonly used as a form of trade restriction by governments. A tariff is "a tax, or duty, levied on a commodity when it crosses the boundary of a customs area." A customs area usually coincides with national political boundaries.[2]

Transfer pricing policies can be used to reduce tariffs imposed on imports into the country or exports outside the country, and, consequently, the cost for a MNE will be less. However, foreign countries may feel that they are losing their revenues because of the manipulations of the transfer pricing policies of MNEs, and they may not accept the transfer price set by the MNE if it is too far from reality.

Any country can use a tariff or duty as a tool to exercise control over goods transferred out of or into the country. If the tariff is imposed by the country on outgoing goods, it is called an export duty; if it is imposed on incoming goods, it is called an import duty.

Governments impose tariffs on imports and exports for three main purposes: (1) to raise revenue for the government; (2) to control the direction of foreign trade; and (3) to protect domestic production against foreign competition. In less developed countries, providing a source of revenue for the government is ranked as the most important purpose of imposing tariffs. In developed countries, such as the United States, tariffs are used to restrict and control the import of goods.

In general, governments can affect the international trade of specific products through the differentiations of tariff rates. High tariffs can be imposed on products that a country does not want to import, and low tariffs or zero tariffs may be imposed on essential products that are badly needed for the national economy.

In international business the effect of tariffs on MNEs' transfer pricing policies varies depending upon the particular country. For countries that depend upon foreign materials or finished goods, import tariffs may be low, and consequently, MNEs may be encouraged to transfer more goods to their foreign subsidiaries domiciled in these countries. On the opposite side are countries whose national products must compete against foreign imports. Governments, under these circumstances, impose high tariffs on imports of certain products to protect their own national products. MNEs may try to overcome these additional costs of paying high tariffs by using low transfer prices on their goods transferred into these countries.

However, MNEs do not have absolute freedom in using different transfer pricing policies for identical goods transferred into two different countries, because if foreign governments discover the differing policies, a conflict between MNEs and host-country governments may be created. As a result, governments may intervene by taking certain actions such as expropriations or the imposition of heavy fines on MNEs who do not use the arm's-length price.

Foreign Exchange Rates

The exchange rate of any country is the economic indicator of how strong or weak the economy is. It provides the link between the national economy and the rest of the world economy. Any economic event, such as bankruptcy of one of the major banks in the country or a large deficit in the balance of payments for the second or third year in a row, has a direct impact on the country's exchange rate. Foreign trade policy, for example, affects the exchange rate directly when the supply or the demand for a country's products moves up or down.

The country's budget is considered to be one of the key factors for MNEs to make their own predictions of the government's intentions regarding tax laws and regulations, foreign exchange control policy, cash movement restriction policy, and any other variables that may affect the country's currency in the short or long run. The budget of the country can show the direction in which the economy may move. It indicates tariff policy, foreign trade policy, tax policy, foreign defense policy, government spending, and many other budget decisions that may have a direct impact on currency markets.[3]

Inflation is one of the key indicators of internal currency depreciation of a country, a fact that may lead to external currency depreciation. There is no perfect direct relationship between inflation and currency devaluation; the relationship is usually indirect and takes time to become clearly evident.[4]

MNEs must take all the above factors into consideration when designing their international transfer pricing policies to assure that their objectives can be achieved within the appropriate pricing policies.

Balance of Payments

Balance of payments summarizes all the economic transactions between the home country and the rest of the world. These transactions include goods and services, transfer payments, loans, and investments. Inflation and interest rates, national income growth, and changes in money supply have a significant impact on the country's currency and its present and future exchange rates. All these factors may affect the balance of payments.

The balance of payments shows the net effect of all currency transactions of a country over a given period of time. When the balance of payments shows a deficit over a period of several years, it is an indication of the likely weakening of the value of the country's currency. This will be a threat to the currency's stability, and it is more likely that the currency will be devaluated.

Deficits and surpluses in the balance of payments affect a country's currency in different ways. National income, money supply, prices, employment, interest rates, and foreign exchange rates are among the most important variables that are usually affected by a deficit or surplus.

MNEs should be aware that when the foreign country's balance of payments shows deficits one year after the other, the foreign government is probably considering one or more of its tools to correct or reduce its deficit. Therefore, MNEs should be alert for restrictive monetary or fiscal policies, such as currency or trade controls, for the purpose of currency devaluation or to control inflation.[5] MNEs may change their international transfer pricing policies to alleviate the impact of the new national policy of a country on their cash movements, the value of goods or services transferred into or out of the country, and the foreign exchange risk.

SOCIOLOGICAL ENVIRONMENTAL FACTORS

Sociological environmental factors include cultural and religious mores, attitudes toward growth and stability, and other societal values. These international sociological constraints interact with international political, legal, and economic environmental factors. Emotional feelings, for example, of a country toward foreigners may lead to laws, rules, restrictions, or regulations that significantly affect the business firms operating abroad.[6] The feelings and attitudes of people in a given country are reflected in the regulations and rules that that country has established with respect to foreign subsidiary operations.

Some of these variables may have an impact on the financial control systems of MNEs investing in different countries, and each may affect the nature and degree of success of MNE control systems required in each host-country environment.[7] MNEs must, therefore, consider seriously all sociological variables and their impact on foreign operations when designing their international transfer pricing policies. They need to direct their attention toward what events might change the underlying social feelings and attitudes of people, which in turn would lead the political groups to alter their current tax and tariff laws, foreign exchange controls, and many other regulations to new and different ones under different national policies. As a result of any change that might occur in the current laws and regulations, MNEs must alter their transfer pricing policies to achieve their major objectives.

POLITICAL AND LEGAL ENVIRONMENTAL FACTORS

Political and legal environmental factors include price controls, government instability, changes of political groups or government, timing of elections, nature of elections, and confiscation of local operations. All these variables can create a high degree of risk or uncertainty, alter the investment climate, and have a significant effect on MNEs' international transfer pricing policies.

It is important that MNEs know how legal constraints and political actions of a given country directly affect their international transfer pricing policies. Since each country is independent, "it is expected that each will have a somewhat different legal structure than others, and that politics of one country will also have different impacts than those of other countries."[8]

Allocation of resources is a potential source of conflict. On the one hand, the home office of the MNE wishes to exercise control measures over the utilization of its resources in foreign countries in order to assure that these resources are used efficiently and profitably. On the other hand, the host country seeks to control the resources of MNEs to make sure that they are used in the national interest.[9] As a result, the government of the host country may interfere by imposing protective measures that can prevent a foreign subsidiary from managing its operations efficiently.

To understand the long-term political stability of a given country, MNEs must look beyond the present government situation to the one that is expected if and when the leadership changes hands.[10] In designing international transfer pricing policies, MNEs may have difficulties in predicting the movement of the political factors and the impact of these factors on their policies. Even so, they must consider these factors and incorporate them into their systems.

SUMMARY

Three different groups of environmental factors in the international market are discussed in this chapter: economic, sociological, and political-legal factors. The most significant economic factors affecting transfer pricing decisions are inflation, tariffs and duties, fluctuations in exchange rates, balance of payments disequilibriums, and restrictions of foreign trade policies. Sociological environmental factors include cultural and religious mores, attitudes toward growth and stability, and many other societal values. Political-legal factors include price controls, government instability, changes of political groups or governments, timing of elections, nature of elections, and confiscation of local operations. MNEs must take all these environmental factors into consideration when designing their international transfer pricing policies and must incorporate them into their systems to assure that their internal and external objectives can be met.

NOTES

1. American Accounting Association, "Report of the Committee on International Accounting," *Accounting Review* 48 (1973 Supplement): 131.

2. Stefan H. Robock and Kenneth Simmonds, *International Business and Multinational Enterprises,* 3rd ed. (Homewood, Ill.: Richard D. Irwin, 1983), 138.

3. Business International Corporation, *Forecasting Foreign Exchange Rates*, Management Monograph 55 (New York: Business International Corporation, 1972), 16.

4. Ibid., 17.

5. Donald A. Ball and Wendell H. McCulloch, Jr., *International Business*, 2nd ed. (Plano, Tex.: Business Publications, 1985), 281.

6. Richard N. Farmer and Barry M. Richman, *International Business*, 3rd ed. (Bloomington, Ind.: Cedarwood Press, 1980), 167.

7. American Accounting Association, "Report of the Committee" (1973): 175.

8. Farmer and Richman, *International Business*, 185.

9. American Accounting Association, "Report of the Committee" (1973): 124.

10. Yain Aharoni and Clifford Baden, *Business in the International Environment*, (Boulder, Co.: West-view Press, 1977): 62.

8

Summary and Conclusions

The purpose of this chapter is to present a summary of international transfer pricing (ITP) policies as guidelines in the decision-making process for executives and businessmen of MNEs in setting up their ITP systems and to state the major conclusions. The chapter begins with a brief summary of the four major characteristics of ITP systems. In the next section the objectives of ITP systems are reviewed. The following sections are comprised of ITP techniques, managerial decision making, tax systems, and environmental factors in the international market and their effects on ITP policies. In the final section, the major conclusions and implications for MNEs' executives and businessmen are presented.

MAJOR CHARACTERISTICS OF INTERNATIONAL TRANSFER PRICING SYSTEMS

In designing ITP systems, four major characteristics should be considered:

1. The inputs consist of seven factors considered as important keys in deciding the appropriate price to be charged for goods transferred across the border from one country to another. These inputs are relevant cost information, differential income tax rates, foreign exchange risks, restrictions on cash transfers, tariffs, competition, and inflation rates.

2. The process includes a series of factors affecting the decision to choose the appropriate ITP technique, which should meet specific requirements to achieve the MNE's objectives. Four elements are included in the process: (1) the factors affecting the decision, (2) different techniques to choose from, (3) specific requirements to be met, and (4) the objectives of ITP systems.

3. The objectives include reduction of income taxes, reduction of tariffs or import and/or export duties, minimization of foreign exchange risks, avoidance of a conflict with host governments, management of cash flows, competitiveness in the international market, consistency with the system of performance evaluation, motivation of subsidiary managers, and the achievement of goal congruence.

4. The output of a well-designed ITP system is an appropriate price that will be the optimum one to achieve all of the MNE's objectives.

THE OBJECTIVES OF INTERNATIONAL TRANSFER PRICING SYSTEMS

An ITP system should achieve two differnt groups of objectives. The first group, dealing with internal reporting, includes the following objectives:

1. Performance evaluation of foreign subsidiary managers is based on their contribution to the performance of the MNE as a whole. With the frequent fluctuations of currency values combined with the floating exchange rates system, MNEs face the problem of distorted performance measurements of their subsidaries as profit centers.

2. Motivation of foreign subsidiary managers should encourage them to increase their divisional profits by transferring goods into and out of their areas of responsibility at an appropriate and fair transfer price while at the same time increasing the global profits of their MNEs.

3. Goal congruence can be achieved when the goals of the MNE's managers, so far as feasible, are consistent with the global goals of the MNE.

The second set of objectives, dealing with external reporting, includes the following:

1. Reduction of income taxes can be achieved by transferring goods to countries with low income tax rates at the lowest possible transfer prices, and by transferring goods out of these countries at the highest possible transfer prices. The minimization of income tax liabilities for MNEs has been considered to be the most significant objective in designing ITP policies.

2. Reduction of tariffs is used by MNEs to reduce import or export tariffs and to avoid paying high tariffs to governments, and consequently to reduce their global costs and maximize their global profits.

3. Minimization of foreign exchange rate risk can be achieved by using the appropriate international transfer prices. Transfer pricing is considered to be one of the best ways to minimize foreign exchange losses from currency fluctuations or to shift the losses to another subsidiary by moving assets from one country to another under the floating exchange rates system.

4. Avoidance of a conflict with host countries' governments can be achieved when MNEs do not charge high transfer prices for goods or services transferred, because high prices mean more cash or fund outflows from the country than cash inflows, which will have a direct impact on the country's balance of payments and consequently on its economy.

5. Management of cash flows is a transfer pricing objective for withdrawing cash from foreign countries by raising transfer prices on goods or services transferred to a foreign subsidiary by another within the same MNE.

6. Competitiveness in international markets against other businesses is another objective of ITP systems, achieved by charging a low transfer price for goods shipped into foreign countries to keep foreign subsidiaries competitive with other local businesses.

INTERNATIONAL TRANSFER PRICING TECHNIQUES

Transfer pricing techniques are divided into two major groups: economic and accounting-oriented, and mathematically oriented. Economic and accounting-oriented methods include the market price, cost-based price, cost-plus price, marginal cost, and negotiated price. Market price is the best price to be used for performance evaluation of foreign subsidiary managers, since it motivates managers to act as if they were managing their own business and, consequently, to reduce costs of production and increase their divisional profits. The full-cost technique is in conformity with U.S. generally accepted accounting principles (GAAP) concerning inventory valuation and income determination. A variable cost-based price leads the buying subsidiary to make optimal decisions in the best interest of the MNE as a whole. A negotiated transfer price retains independence of each manager to make the right decision for his or her subsidiary and makes each manager accountable for the outcome of his or her decisions.

Mathematically oriented techniques include linear programming, nonlinear programming, and goal-programming models. The mathematical programming models allocate resources efficiently and, at the same time, evaluate the efficient use of the resources under a decentralized organization.

MANAGERIAL DECISION MAKING IN MNEs

Many different types of managerial decisions require the use of transfer pricing policies, and each decision may need a different pricing technique. Capital budgeting decisions are the only ones discussed in detail in this book.

MNEs need more relevant models for international capital budgeting decisions, which must include the effects of all environmental variables and their impact on the global profits of MNEs. A normative model for capital budgeting decisions of foreign projects using net present value (NPV) techniques is suggested. The model may be considered as a comprehensive one since it includes the effects of inflation, political risk (including expropriation), foreign exchange risk, and the effect of transfer pricing policies on accepting or rejecting the project.

TAXATION OF INTERNATIONAL
INTRACOMPANY TRANSFERS

ITP decisions have a significant impact on the international operations of MNEs, directly affecting their global profits, and can help or limit MNEs' ability to operate, manage, and utilize their economic resources on a global basis for the purpose of achieving their ultimate goals.

Section 482 of the U.S. Internal Revenue Code of the 1986 Tax Reform Act has focused on the concept of comparing intra group transfer prices with arm's-length intracompany third-party prices. Section 482 insists that intracompany transactions be priced at arm's length, or as if they involved unrelated parties in the open market.

In Canada the federal government imposes a 46 percent tax rate on Canadian based MNEs. In the United Kingdom all U.K.-based MNEs are liable for a tax rate of 35 percent on their worldwide profits. In West Germany the profits of German-based MNEs are taxed at the rate of 56 percent for the undistributed profits and 36 percent for the distributed earnings. In Japan MNEs are required to aggregate the loss or income of foreign branches with income tax or loss of the corporation and pay the Japanese corporate income tax of 33.3 percent on distributed income or 43.3 percent on undistributed income on their worldwide income.

Environmental factors in the international markets include: economic, sociological, and political legal factors. Inflation, tariffs, and duties, fluctuations in exchange rate, balance of payment disequilibirum, and restrictions of foreign trade policies affecting transfer pricing policies of MNEs.

Sociological factors; such as cultural and religious mores, attitudes toward growth and stability, and many other societal values; and political-legal factors; such as price controls, government instability, and change of political groups among others; must be taken into consideration by MNEs when designing their ITP policies and must incorporate them into their systems to assure that their objectives can be met.

CONCLUSIONS AND IMPLICATIONS

The basic purpose of this book is to establish guidelines for MNEs' executives and businessmen in designing the appropriate international transfer pricing system, which should

1. provide relevant and timely information for MNEs' headquarters to use as guidelines in managerial decision making;
2. improve the global profits of MNEs;
3. motivate foreign subsidiary managers to achieve the highest possible profits of subsidiaries in harmony with the MNE's overall objectives; and

4. minimize the international transaction costs for MNEs by minimizing tariffs, income tax liabilities in both home and host countries, foreign exchange risks, currency manipulation losses, and conflicts with foreign countries' governments' policies.

It has been found that MNEs, theoretically, have the ability to use their ITP policies to achieve the highest possible global profits of their domestic and international operations. However, establishing ITP policies is the most difficult and complicated pricing problem that MNEs face. The major conclusions and implications of the research are presented here.

1. For the reduction of both income tax liabilities and tariffs, as long as the tax rate differential is higher than the net effect of the tariff rate imposed by the country with the higher tax rate, the higher transfer price will always generate net savings for the MNEs. However, if the higher transfer price results in showing artificial losses for the buying subsidiary, the net effect will be deterimental for the MNE as a whole because the total income tax liabilities and tariffs to be paid will always be more than with lower transfer prices.

2. With the fluctuations in foreign exchange rates, assets in weak currencies can be moved through the use of higher transfer prices. However, the intervention of host-country governments with or without price controls will certainly limit the MNE's ability to use this technique.

3. When performance evaluation is combined with fluctuations in foreign exchange rates, transfer pricing policies may lead to presenting misleading and imperfect financial measures of performance.

4. When MNEs try to achieve motivation, goal congruence, and autonomy of foreign subsidiary managers, they may create conflicting results with performance evaluation, reduction of income taxes, reduction of tariffs, and avoidance of foreign exchange risks. However, when different objectives lead to conflicting results, MNEs have to make trade-offs between achieving different objectives and must be satisfied with lower global profits when one objective has a priority over others, especially in the case of long-run objectives.

5. MNEs are in urgent need of a practical and objective technique or model that can avoid conflicts between different objectives of the system and, at the same time, achieve the global goals of MNEs to continue doing their international business under different economic, sociological, and political environmental conditions.

6. The significance of fast change in environmental conditions, such as market conditions, government attitudes, and differential global strategies, forces MNEs to use different transfer prices at different times under different conditions.

7. The use of any transfer price other than the arm's-length price is unacceptable to tax authorities of the United States and most industrially developed countries.

8. For capital budgeting decisions, MNEs should consider the effects of foreign exchange rate fluctuations, inflation in foreign countries where projects are expected to be located, political risks, and the effect of different ITP policies, which will lead them to make optimum capital budgeting decisions by choosing the best alternative that will help them in achieving their global objectives in the long run.

9. A modified and comprehensive net present value (NPV) technique is suggested for use by MNEs in making their capital budgeting decisions. The suggested technique includes the effect of four different factors: (1) foreign exchange rate fluctuations, (2) inflation in foreign countries where the projects are expected to be located, (3) transfer pricing policies, and (4) political risks.

10. In designing the appropriate ITP system, MNEs must take the effect of different environmental factors, that is, economic, sociological, and political-legal variables, into consideration to assure that their internal as well as external objectives can be achieved.

Appendix A

Internal Revenue Code Section 482, Allocation of Income and Deductions among Taxpayers

In any case of two or more organizations, trades, or businesses (whether or not incorporated, whether or not organized in the United States, and whether or not affiliated) owned or controlled directly or indirectly by the same interests, the Secretary may distribute, apportion, or allocate gross income, deductions, credits, or allowances between or among such organizations, trades, or businesses, if he determines that such distribution, apportionment, or allocation is necessary in order to prevent evasion of taxes or clearly to reflect the income of any of such organizations, trades, or businesses.

In the case of any transfer (or license) of intangible property (within the meaning of section 936(h)(3)(B)), the income with respect to such transfer or license shall be commensurate with the income attributable to the intangible.

Amendments

P.L. 99-514, § 1231(e)(1):

Act Sec. 1231(e)(1) amended Code Sec. 482 by adding at the end thereof a new sentence to read as above.

The above amendment applies to tax years beginning after December 31, 1986. However, see Act Sec. 1231(g)(2)-(4), below.

Act Sec. 1231(g)(2)-(4) provides:

(2) SPECIAL RULE FOR TRANSFER OF INTANGIBLES.—

(A) IN GENERAL.—The amendments made by subsection (e) shall apply to taxable years beginning after December 31, 1986, but only with respect to transfers after November 16, 1985, or licenses granted after such date (or before such date with respect to property not in existence or owned by the taxpayer on such date).

(B) SPECIAL RULE FOR SECTION 936.—For purposes of section 936(h)(5)(C) of the Internal Revenue Code of 1986 the amendments made by subsection (e) shall apply to taxable years beginning after December 31, 1986, without regard to when the transfer (or license) was made.

(3) SUBSECTION (f).—The amendment made by subsection (f) shall apply to taxable years beginning after December 31, 1982.

(4) TRANSITIONAL RULE.—In the case of a corporation—

(A) with respect to which an election under section 936 of the Internal Revenue Code of 1986 (relating to possessions tax credit) is in effect,

(B) which produced an end-product form in Puerto Rico on or before September 3, 1982,

(C) which began manufacturing a component of such product in Puerto Rico in its taxable year beginning in 1983, and

(D) with respect to which a Puerto Rican tax exemption was granted on June 27, 1983, such corporation shall treat such component as a separate product for such taxable year for purposes of determining whether such corporation had a significant business presence in Puerto Rico with respect to such product and its income with respect to such product.

Amended 1954 Code by substituting "Secretary" for "Secretary or his delegate" each place it appeared. Effective February 1, 1977.

Code Sec. 482. Allocation of Income and Deductions Among Taxpayers

¶ 4410   The IRS has the power to apportion income and deductions among two or more organizations, trades or businesses that are owned or controlled, directly or indirectly, by the same interests. This power is discretionary and is not limited to corporations. It is applicable to businesses owned by individuals or partnerships, and to any class of organization (.05). An individual's activities also have been deemed to be a trade or business to which income may be allocated (.07). Where an existing business is divided up into multiple corporations, the restrictions on controlled corporations should also be considered (see ¶ 6173 and 6181-6187).

Control, for purposes of income and deduction allocation, is not limited to stock ownership. Any kind of control is relevant, regardless of whether or not it is legally enforceable control (.10). Businesses, however, are not controlled by the same interests merely because relatives own a controlling interest in each (.12).

● Basis for IRS action

By statute, the IRS must determine that an allocation is necessary (1) to prevent the evasion of taxes or (2) to clearly reflect the income of the related taxpayers. Thus, where

1639-12   Adjustments

parties to a transaction seek to avoid the tax laws, the IRS has the power to reallocate tax attributes in order to defeat this intention. For example, when a parent merges a subsidiary into itself as part of a tax-free liquidation and claims losses on assets held by the subsidiary, the IRS may reallocate the losses to the subsidiary in order to prevent the corporation from enjoying the double tax benefit of income earned by the assets and losses claimed upon their disposition (.13).

The authority of the IRS to allocate income is not limited to acts of fraud, sham transactions, or devices to avoid tax. It also covers situations where true taxable income is not reported because the transaction did not take place at arm's length. For example, where a bargain sale is consummated between two corporations owned by the same individual, the seller's income is increased to reflect the arm's-length price, the basis of the property in the buyer's hands is similarly increased, and the sole stockholder is treated as having received a dividend from the seller and having made a capital contribution to the buyer (.15). The allocation rules are also applicable where there is a bargain sale of property by two subsidiaries to their common parent, even though the parent may have realized no gain on the disposition of the property to the shareholders (.155). Also, when a parent corporation receives a stock dividend from its subsidiary and then donates the stock to a charitable foundation, the IRS may reallocate the charitable deduction to the subsidiary (.16). Furthermore, reallocation of income was appropriate where a subsidiary charged a parent a below-market price for the right to market the subsidiary's patented products (.163).

A determination by the IRS to allocate income between a corporation and its controlling shareholder/employee may only be set aside if it is arbitrary and the transactions were not made at arm's-length (.165).

The IRS was not required to make a corresponding reduction in the taxes of a lessor corporation when rental deductions that were claimed by a related lessee corporation were denied. Interestingly, instead of basing its assessment upon its allocation authority, the IRS based the assessment on Code Sec. 162, which disallows deductions for unreasonable rental payments (.17).

The regulations provide guidelines for allocations between corporations and their subsidiaries (including foreign affiliates) relating to loans or advances, performance of services for another, use of tangible property, transfer or use of intangible property, and sales of tangible property (.18).

● "Safe haven" interest rates

Interest should be charged on loans or advances made by one member of a controlled group to another. If the creditor is regularly engaged in the business of making loans or advances, an arm's-length interest rate should be charged. If the creditor fails to do so, the IRS can determine what interest should have been charged. Where the creditor is not in the business of loaning money or making advances, either an arm's-length rate based on the facts and circumstances or a "safe haven" rate is acceptable.

If a creditor is not regularly engaged in the business of making loans or advances, a safe-haven zone of at least 11 percent but not more than 13 percent simple interest will satisfy the arm's-length requirement. If the interest charged by the controlled group member falls outside of this zone, and if the creditor is otherwise unable to establish a valid arm's-length rate, the IRS may set up an allocation reflecting a rate of 12 percent simple interest a year. These rates apply to interest paid or accrued pursuant to a loan or advance entered into after June 30, 1981 (other than a loan or advance entered into pursuant to a binding contract entered into before August 29, 1980). They also apply to interest paid or accrued after June 30, 1981, pursuant to a demand loan or advance.

The regulations that provide the above "safe haven" interest rates are to be amended to provide "safe haven" interest rates for *sales* between commonly controlled organizations, trades or businesses that are consistent with the original issue discount rates (see ¶ 4420) (.20).

● **Creation of income**

The allocation rules may be utilized even where there is no clearly existing income. For instance, interest income may be allocated on noninterest-bearing notes where the loans between the controlled taxpayers would not have been made on an interest-free basis in arm's-length dealings between unrelated taxpayers (.22).

In keeping with this arm's-length standard, the IRS did not have to reallocate, among all the subsidiaries of a finance group, the interest charges on loans by the parent where the parent charged interest only to those subsidiaries that did not have impaired capital (.30). The IRS was permitted to impute interest only to those subsidiaries with impaired capital, as this more closely conformed the parent's interest income to the arm's-length standard.

● **Professional and service corporations**

The IRS has the power to allocate income between a professional service corporation and its employee-owners in order to prevent tax avoidance. See ¶ 3522.

● **Post-November 16, 1985, transfers of intangibles**

Generally, for tax years beginning after 1986, income allocations with respect to post-November 16, 1985, transfers of intangible property or the right to use such property are to be commensurate with the income attributable to the intangible. For these transfers, the arm's-length standard will no longer provide a safe harbor. This rule applies to transfers between U.S. and foreign organizations, trades or businesses.

.01 Reg. §§ 1.482-1. 1.482-2.

.05 *J.T.Williams*, 47 TCM 846, CCH Dec. 40,915(M), TC Memo. 1983-770.

.07 *T.B. Fegan*, 71 TC 791, CCH Dec. 35,880.

.10 *Advance Machinery Exchange, Inc.*, CA-2, 52-1 USTC ¶ 66,036, 196 F2d 1006; *B. Forman Co., Inc.*, CA-2, 72-1 USTC ¶ 9182, 453 F2d 1144, rev'g TC, 54 TC 912, CCH Dec. 30,087 (Nonacq.), cert. den., 407 U.S. 934.

.12 *R. Brittingham*, CA-5, 79-2 USTC ¶ 9499; *Dallas Ceramic Co.*, CA-5, 79-2 USTC ¶ 9500.

.13 *General Electric Co.*, ClsCt, 83-2 USTC ¶ 9532.

.15 Rev. Rul. 69-630, 1969-2 CB 112.

.155 IRS Letter Ruling 7927009, 3-22-79.

.16 *Northwestern National Bank of Minneapolis*, CA-8, 77-2 USTC ¶ 9479, 556 F2d 889.

.163 *Eli Lilly and Co.*, 84 TC 996, CCH Dec. 42,113.

.165 *S. Achiro*, 77 TC 881, CCH Dec. 38,351.

.17 *OTM Corporation*, CA-5, 78-1 USTC ¶ 9430, 572 F2d 1046, affirming per curiam DC Tex., 77-2 USTC ¶ 9693.

.18 Reg. § 1.482.

.20 Sec. 44(b) of the Tax Reform Act of 1984 (P.L. 98-369).

.22 *B. Forman Co., Inc.* CA-2, 72-1 USTC ¶ 9182, 453 F2d 1144, cert. den., 407 U.S. 934; *Kahler Corp.*, CA-8, 73-2 USTC ¶ 9687, 486 F2d 1; *Kerry Investment Co.*, CA-9, 74-2 USTC ¶ 9522, 500 F2d 108; *Fitzgerald Motor Co.*, CA-5, 75-1 USTC ¶ 9275, 508 F2d 1096; *Latham Park Manor, Inc.*, 69 TC 199, CCH Dec. 34,733.

.30 *Liberty Loan Corp.*, CA-8, 74-1 USTC ¶ 9474, 498 F2d 225, rev'g and rem'g DC, 73-1 USTC ¶ 9416, 359 FSupp 158, cert. den., 419 U.S. 1089.

Appendix B

Management Accounting Guidelines on Interunit Transfer Pricing Issued by the Institute of Cost and Management Accountants (ICMA, London)

I am pleased to introduce the first of a series of Management Accounting Guidelines which are being published under the auspices of the Research and Technical Committee. The Institute was not in favour of introducing Management Accounting Standards, preferring to issue Guidelines based on best practice and thereby leaving their use to the discretion of members, in the light of the relevant circumstances.

AUSTIN CALLAGHAN
President

September 1981

This appendix originally appeared as *Management Accountant Guidelines*, No. 1: "Inter-unit Transfer Pricing" (October 1981), published by The Institute of Cost and Management Accountants.

MANAGEMENT ACCOUNTING GUIDELINES

Inter-unit Transfer Pricing

Contents

Introduction
Where a unit of a company makes a product which another unit incorporates in its production process, the price at which the product is transferred can be important to the well-being of both units and the company as a whole. The importance of the transfer pricing mechanism employed in relation to criteria such as divisional autonomy, objective performance evaluation and the congruence of the aims of central and divisional management will continue to grow as organisations grow. The guideline which follows considers the factors involved and tries to define the characteristics of an optimal transfer pricing policy.

1. The background
As a result of a large number of business mergers and acquisitions which have taken place in recent years there has been a tendency for business organisations to increase in complexity. At the same time there has been a spread in the use of decentralisation or divisionalisation as a means of controlling large companies. As some of these large companies have been created from the fusion of several smaller businesses, in some instances the situation has now arisen in which companies are attempting to derive the maximum benefit from their overall size, whilst at the same time trying to take full advantage of the smallness of the units of which they are composed.

Whilst the economies to be derived from large scale production and distribution are evident in many industries, it is generally agreed that the successful management of any organisation by a central group of people becomes increasingly difficult as that organisation grows in size and spreads geographically. Decentralisation in one form or another to a greater or lesser extent is therefore often the solution. This decision to decentralise is often reflected in a variety of benefits to the organisation as a whole, largely it is claimed because the manager of the decentralised unit has a greater incentive to succeed if he is made responsible for the profitability of his unit, as opposed to being responsible for its cost performance only, the situation which normally exists in an organisation where control remains centralised.

However, decentralisation often also brings a number of problems which are not present in centrally controlled organisations. One of the most important problems arises where a substantial part of the output of one unit is transferred to another division within the same organisation and a pricing structure has to be determined in respect of the transfer. Some form of inter-unit pricing system has to be constructed, because the assessment of the profitability of each unit is a necessary factor in any policy of decentralisation. In addition to ensuring that the pricing system is equitable as far as the individual units are concerned, consideration must also be given to its effect on overall company policy and the profitability of the organisation as a whole. Where central management wishes to ensure that the objectives of its divisional managers remain in accord with overall company policy, that objective performance evaluation of these managers is retained and that the units retain the high degree of autonomy necessary to maintain a decentralised situation, careful consideration must be given to the difficulties involved in the creation and operation of the inter-unit pricing mechanism.

For example, a division supplying another with a product which the receiving division will process further, may be in the position of a monopolist supplier. By taking advantage of its own position it could hold the division it supplies to ransom. The management at headquarters could perhaps afford to take a detached view of the situation if the amount which the transferor division could add to its own profit merely offset the diminution in the profit of the transferee division. But it is possible for the buying division to lose more than the selling division gains, meaning that the profits of the organisation as a whole will be adversely affected.

For example, Division A of a company is the sole supplier of a product which Division B of the same company processes further before sale to outside customers.

If a part of Division A's costs is fixed, then its total costs per day will increase as its volume of production increases but not as quickly. If we assume:

(a) that its total costs are £250 per day for any output up to 500 units per day and that total costs increase by £50 per day for every additional 500 units made, and

(b) that the manager of this division has decided that his operating results will be optimised if he sets his selling price to Division B at £0.30 per unit (i.e. his transfer price at £0.30 per unit),

the relevant figures will be as shown in Table I.

TABLE I

Division A's transfers to Division B (in units)	Value of Division A's transfers to Division B (at £0.30 per unit) £	Divisions A's total cost £	Divisions A's profit £
500	150	250	(100)
1,000	300	300	—
1,500	450	350	100
2,000	600	400	200
2,500	750	450	300
3,000	900	500	400

Similarly if we assume:

(a) that Division B incurs processing costs of £625 for any output up to 500 units per day, and £125 per 500 for outputs in excess of 500, and

(b) that Division B's selling price per unit to outside customers declines as the volume of sales increases,

the situation will be as shown in Table II.

TABLE II

Div. B sales (units)	Div. A's charge to Div. B (or sub-assembly at 30p per unit) £	Div. B's processing costs £	Total costs £	Div. B's selling price (per unit) £	Total £	Div. B's profit or loss £
500	150	625	775	1.50	750	(25)
1000	300	750	1,050	1.25	1,250	200
1500	450	875	1,325	1.10	1,650	325
2000	600	1,000	1,600	1.00	2,000	400
2500	750	1,125	1,875	0.90	2,250	375
3000	900	1,250	2,150	0.70	2,100	(50)

It can be seen from Table II that the most profitable policy for Division B is to set its output at 2,000 units per day, thereby earning a profit of £400 per day. If Division A supplies 2,000 units per day to Division B, Division A's sales will be worth £600 and its total costs £400. Its profits will be £200, giving a total profit for the company as a whole of £600.

However, it can also be seen from Table I that a greater demand from Division B, i.e. 3,000 units per day rather than only 2,000 units per day, would have resulted in an increased profit for Division A. However, the manager of Division B will not increase his demand because, as Table II shows, such a decision will operate against his personal interests.

If instead of having two profit centres, the company abandons its divisionalised structure and combines both divisions into a single profit centre, the situation would be as shown in Table III.

TABLE III

Output (in units)	Cost of producing sub-assembly £	Cost of processing to completion £	Total cost £	Total sales £	Profit £
500	250	625	875	750	(125)
1,000	300	750	1,050	1,250	200
1,500	350	875	1,225	1,650	425
2,000	400	1,000	1,400	2,000	600
2,500	450	1,125	1,575	2,250	675
3,000	500	1,250	1,750	2,100	350

It can be seen that the single profit centre will operate more profitably than the two divisions together – by making and selling 2,500 units per day, it can earn a profit of £675 as opposed to £600 when the company is decentralised.

In the original decentralised situation, Division B's management has reacted to the transfer price of £0.30 per unit by restricting its demand for the sub-assembly and therefore its own output of the finished product. An unsatisfactory result has been created for the company as a whole, yet if the divisional manager has been following an instruction to maximise his division's separate profit, he has fulfilled his objective.

It may therefore be assumed that it is Division A's management who have been responsible for the overall profit falling below the optimum, yet here again the divisional management cannot be faulted for it established a transfer price of £0.30 per unit in the belief that sales at that price would produce a better divisional profit than an increased level of sales at a smaller price. It is important to note that the transfer price in such a situation from the viewpoint of the supplying division, has been constructed on the basis of variable cost plus an element to cover fixed cost plus profit, yet as far as the purchasing division is concerned it is a wholly variable cost – the total cost of the sub-assemblies purchased from Division A will vary directly with the number of units purchased.

The outcome of situations such as that illustrated in the example might lead to a questioning of the validity of a policy of decentralisation where there is a considerable volume of interdivisional trading. It might be felt that the price paid for the luxury of divisionalisation is excessive, and that the most profitable outcome would be a reversion to a policy of centralisation. The volume of losses arising from the circumstances outlined (sub-optimisation) would, however, have to be very high before the benefits of decentralisation would be given up.

Transfer prices may therefore be viewed as constraints on decentralisation because they are designed to link at least two divisions or sub-systems, whereas by definition all sub-systems in a totally decentralised system should act as though they were independent. At its extreme, decentralisation means complete freedom to make local decisions in the best interests of a sub-unit as if the unit were independent.

The major cost of such decentralisation is this *dysfunctional* decision-making, e.g. buying outside when purchases should be made inside.

2. Criteria for developing transfer prices

It would appear that an inter-unit pricing method must meet several requirements which reach into the very heart of the decentralised operation. These requirements must be satisfied if the organisation is to achieve its potential level of efficiency. First in importance is that the inter-unit pricing method must arrive at a competitive price. This is basic to the entire structure of decentralisation. Profits are the yardstick for the measurement of managerial ability. If inter-unit profits are not natural, i.e. competitive, this important means of evaluating management will be lost.

Top management must use divisional income statements in arriving at policy decisions concerning the profitability of divisional ventures. The decision to make or subcontract various component parts of the company's end product will certainly be greatly influenced by the apparent profit or loss of a particular division. It is even possible that a decision to continue or to terminate operations of a division may depend on results based on inter-unit transfer prices.

Inter-unit pricing may well play a major part in showing a profit or a loss for a particular division. Unless top management is to ignore inter-unit statements and go back to rule of thumb decisions in these matters an inter-unit pricing system must be established which –

(a) fosters a healthy inter-departmental competitive spirit, without needless arguments,
(b) provides an adequate profit yardstick for departmental management, and
(c) provides figures to top management for use in policy decisions, e.g. to make or to subcontract.

Having established the criteria which are required for the development of transfer prices, consideration should then be given to various company policies which have been adopted to govern transfers from one division to another within the same organisation.

3. Company policies governing inter-unit transfers
A number of years ago in the United States a study of company policies governing inter-unit transfers reached the following conclusions:
1. Internal procurement is expected where the company's products and services are superior or equal in design, quality, performance and price, when acceptable delivery schedules can be met, the receiving unit suffers no loss and the supplier unit's profit accrues to the company.

Often the receiving unit gains advantages such as better control over quality, assurance of continued supply and prompt delivery. If a receiving unit finds that internal sources of supply are not competitive, policy calls for one of the following actions:

(a) It may purchase from an outside supplier after it has made a reasonable effort to bring the internal supplier unit's quotations and terms into line with those available outside.

(b) It is free to purchase outside but must be prepared to justify its decision. Central executives usually review such actions and have an opportunity to take action where needed. Normally the right to buy outside is seldom used because the advantages of integration make inter-unit transfers preferable for both supplying and receiving units. Companies interviewed stated that the policy had sometimes been instrumental in bringing to light the presence of excessive costs due to obsolete or poorly located facilities, inefficient management, lack of volume or other causes. In some cases it is customary to split purchases between internal and external suppliers because internal capacity is inadequate or because management wishes to have alternative sources available.

2. Transfer prices are expected to be competitive, but internal procurement is required or necessary because no satisfactory outside source is available. Where competitive prices are not profitable to the supplier unit, central executive and staff facilities are utilised to formulate and put into effect the plan for improvement. Internal transfer policies applying to different products often vary according to the nature of the product and conditions under which it is marketed and sold.

4. Significance in decision making
The importance of pricing mechanisms employed in the transfer of products from one division to another division within the same company lies in their effect on the motivation of the divisional management and in consequence, on the overall profitability of the organisation. Incorrectly based transfer prices may motivate divisional managers to take decisions which, whilst apparently in the best interests of the divisions for which they are responsible, would not be taken by central management in the same circumstances because of their adverse effect on the level of overall company profits.

Where divisional managers and central management are motivated differently, the transfer pricing system is dysfunctional and may lead to suboptimisation – the situation in which the quantity of output of the supplying unit accepted by the purchasing unit is different from the optimal level. The circumstances existing in any particular situation must therefore be reviewed and considered carefully before the transfer pricing system is implemented. Otherwise the benefits of decentralisation will not be realised in full, or decisions taken by a divisional manager without full information relating to all of the factors involved may create a loss in another division which exceeds his profit and will consequently lower the overall profit.

There are however, dangers in the arbitrary imposition of transfer prices by central management because this can destroy the autonomy of the divisional management and thereby the profit incentive which appears to encourage them to increase the level of production more than any incentive based on cost. It has been found that where divisions which formerly operated as cost centres are converted into profit centres, management continues to worry about costs, but also gives greater consideration than before to methods of boosting production and to the needs of its customers. As a result, central managements are often more successful in achieving goal congruence (ensuring that the objectives of their divisional managers are the same as their own) through such profit centres than through cost centres. The advocates of profit may often therefore be correct in maintaining that the responsibility for profit centre performance provides more incentive than being responsible for cost performance, because increasing profits by improving sales performance is much more rewarding than meeting budgeted costs. In a number of instances it has been recognised that if profit control is operated on a centralised basis no one at divisional level is greatly concerned if an improvement in quality involves additional costs. The divisional manager obtains budget authorisation to offset the increased costs, the burden of the quality control department is eased and the sales force have a product which is easier to market. Even when these personnel are aware that the increased quality is not reflected in an increase in the selling price of the finished product and that the company is therefore wasting money, in a centralised profit control situation there is little incentive for any of them to take steps to eliminate this cost.

Profit maximisation is, however, open to at least two interpretations. It is likely that a divisional manager whose managerial abilities are assessed at least partially by the profit performance of his unit will be concerned with short-run profit maximisation, whereas his central management may take a longer view. If promotion prospects and salary increases are dependent on present performance, the divisional manager may take decisions which will enhance the short-run profitability of his unit but may have an adverse effect on future profits of the division, possibly after he has moved on. Difficulties may therefore arise in assessing long term managerial performance if central management permits divisional heads to become too preoccupied with the present situation and allow them to ignore the long term objectives of the organisation as a whole.

5. Constraints on the degree of divisional autonomy
Nevertheless, it is clear that the establishment of a profit centre is not always the solution to the problem. A pricing mechanism which can be influenced by personalities and corporate decisions may prove so unsuccessful that a return to a cost basis which eliminates the overhead costs incurred by staff engaged in transfer price disputes would be beneficial. Even more important, situations do exist in which the creation of profit centres is illogical. Where a supplying unit and a purchasing unit are so closely linked that they must trade, there being no satisfactory outside alternatives, the establishment of these units as independent profit centres is probably an example of self-deception on the part of the management. In such instances management control by means of a system of predetermined standard costs must be more realistic. Besides being less harrowing to the divisional staff because of the elimination of the arguments which are inevitable in a captive buyer or seller situation, cost control, involving the comparison of actual costs with predetermined standard costs, enables central management to evaluate the performance of their divisional managers. Management by exception, the practice of investigating large variances from the predetermined standard, is widely recognised as a valuable aid to management control.

There are, other costs however, which cannot be classified as engineered costs because there is no scientific way of determining the correct amount which ought to be incurred. These costs can be termed managed costs or discretionary costs, because they can be whatever management wants them to be within fairly wide limits. For example, in the short run a divisional manager may economise on the cost of maintenance and repairs without detriment to the operation of the plant for which he is responsible. Prolonged continuation of this policy would ultimately result in breakdowns which could prove expensive in the shape of lost production. Costs of this nature cannot be monitored by a standard cost system and management control and evaluation of performance has therefore to be implemented by some other means. Plant safety, for example, can be checked regularly by a member of head office staff and a register of repairs and maintenance carried out may be subjected to periodical audit by the group maintenance officer. In effect, in divisions operated as cost centres, provision may have to be made to divest divisional management of most of the responsibility for discretionary costs and place the control in the hands of specific members of the head office staff.

6. Transfer pricing in practice

Studies of transfer pricing systems indicate that there is often considerable disparity between the practical applications of transfer pricing mechanisms and what might reasonably be expected from the study of the theoretical analysis of the subject. In some instances there are particular circumstances which account to some degree for this disparity. For example, where an organisation supplies a range of finished products to the outside market and the sales of each are largely dependent on the availability of the other products in the range, transfers of intermediate products or sub-assemblies will continue to take place internally in spite of the fact that these intermediate products might possibly be sold more profitably on the outside market. Similarly, there may be justification in isolated cases for permitting a transfer price which is not economically viable in the short term, in order to maintain the existence of a division, because central management has decided that this unit has a function to perform in the group's long term policy.

Whilst allowing that these explanations will account for some of the vagaries of transfer pricing mechanisms in practice, there are still many cases where the transfer price employed cannot be justified on any' logical basis. There is evidence that managements are influenced by a variety of other factors which may be important in their particular circumstances, but it is disquieting to note that questions relating to the optimal internal transfer price have often never been asked. Many managements are unaware that suboptimisation is occurring within their organisations and that a change in the transfer pricing mechanism could appreciably increase their overall profitability. Even in situations where company policy directs that divisional autonomy may take precedence over every other consideration, it is important that the correct information is available on all of the factors involved before decisions are taken relating to inter-unit trading. Regrettably, results of surveys and case studies carried out on this subject indicate that the quality and quantity of this information is less than might reasonably be expected from many of the management control systems in operation at present. Although it is clear that some of the theoretical arguments advanced in favour of the concept of marginal cost can be applied in practice it would seem that the relevant cost accounting information necessary to benefit from the use of the concept is inadequate in many organisations. If the management accounting systems cannot provide the basic information relating to fixed and variable costs there must be little hope of achieving optimal transfer prices, since they depend on the cost and revenue functions. Whilst it is recognised that companies can only forecast the opportunity cost of inter-unit sales, because they do not know the precise price elasticity of demand for their products, it should not be beyond the powers of their accounting staff to produce reasonably accurate schedules of changes in costs at different volumes of output. Information of this nature and its proper use would at least ensure that companies were moving towards optimal transfer prices.

7. International transfers
It will have been seen from the foregoing that it is often no easy matter to find a rational method for pricing the transfer of products from one unit to another unit within the same

company. Even where both units are operating in the same country difficulties can and do arise, but in a multi-national organisation where one division or corporate subsidiary is located in a different country from the other, additional factors must be taken into account when trying to resolve the problems of control. Considerations relating to the effects of taxation, tariffs, joint venture partnerships etc have to be added to the factors already present in the purely domestic transfer situation, and as a result the difficulties are multiplied.

A. *Taxation*

In international transfers, differing tax rules and rates in the countries in question are probably the most important factor when trying to arrive at an equitable transfer price. Where the transfer price can be adjusted to reduce the taxable income of the organisation in a country where tax rates are high, there must always be some inducement to take advantage of such circumstances. It is not surprising, therefore, that there is evidence of subsidiaries in tax havens being used as intermediaries between related companies which operate in areas of high taxation. As a result governments have found it necessary to introduce legislation which makes it difficult to avoid taxation by adjusting transfer prices. However, it has been claimed that a real danger can arise in multi-national companies because governments have protected their tax base so well that the companies can become subject to double taxation on the same income.

In the USA the Treasury has the authority to reallocate gross income, reductions, credits or allowances between units of the same organisation, to prevent tax evasion or to reflect more clearly a proper allocation of income. If such a re-allocation is made, the burden of proof is on the taxpayer to show that the Treasury has been arbitrary or unreasonable in re-allocating income. Similarly, in some European countries a system known as 'contract processing' is operated by which the taxable income and taxable net worth of foreign-owned companies are negotiated rather than determined by normal accounting practices. In this way the government ensures that the tax charges are not determined by transfer prices which could be manipulated in situations where much of the raw material used is imported and most of the finished product is exported.

B. Tariffs

The tariff rates imposed by the country in which the buying division or corporate subsidiary is located is also a factor to be taken into account in determining transfer prices. In situations where tariffs are based on the value of the product being imported, a lower transfer price will mean a reduced tariff charge. The saving in tariff duty will, however, have to be set off against the increased taxation arising out of higher profits where the difference between the selling price of the finished product and the total cost incurred is higher. Just as most countries are aware of the effect of transfer prices on the revenue from taxation, so also are they aware that artificially low import prices will mean less revenue from tariffs. As a result, it is not uncommon for governments to impose tariffs which are based on arm's length market prices if the transfer prices are much lower. No doubt the possibility of obtaining more revenue from taxation will enter into their calculations but, as there is always the chance that additional costs incurred subsequently will reduce profits and therefore taxation revenue, it may be that they will decide to take the revenue when they can, at the point where the raw materials or semi-finished goods enter the country.

C. Currency fluctuations

Exchange risks arise when a multinational company has assets or liabilities in a foreign currency, whose values in terms of domestic currency decrease following a shift in the exchange rate between the two currencies. The position of the multinational differs significantly from that of the exporter or importer, because all the items in the balance sheets of its overseas subsidiaries are exposed to exchange risk, whereas exporters and importers have only financial claims or debts to meet as a result of trading transactions. In the consolidation of the accounts of the multinational company and its subsidiaries exchange losses can therefore arise in the translation of the balance sheet items of any subsidiary into the domestic currency.

It should be noted that a change in the transfer price does not in itself affect exchange risks. Exchange risks will be affected only when changes in transfer prices are complemented by changes in the timing of payments, i.e. by leading (anticipatory moves) or lagging (delaying techniques). For example, if an amount owing to a selling company is paid before the due date (leading) and thereby occurs before a fall in the currency of the buyer's country, an exchange loss will be averted. Judicious leading or lagging eliminates exchange risk because the party in whose currency the claim is denominated is not affected by exchange fluctuations.

Research has indicated that leading and lagging is the most widespread technique used by multinational companies in avoiding currency risks. Transfer pricing practices can enhance the exchange-risk-avoiding virtues of leading or lagging by inflating the receipts of the companies in strong currency areas from the sections of the group operating in weak currency areas. Funds can be moved out of a weak currency into a stronger currency by the manipulation of transfer prices. However, it should be noted that the benefits arising from such manipulations only arise because the adjustments in transfer pricing have been grafted on to leading or lagging moves.

D. Joint ventures

In a multi-national company, the transfer pricing system may be dysfunctional because the maximisation of profits in a subsidiary company, whilst protecting the interests of the local shareholders in that company, may be sub-optimal from the viewpoint of the organisation as a whole. It has been stated that following a decision to rationalise production on a worldwide basis so that each division would specialise in certain products or components, a major American motor car manufacturer was forced to abandon its policy of working with joint ventures partly because of the transfer pricing problem and, as a result, had to buy out a large European minority interest at a time when the effects of the drain on the US balance of payments could hardly have been worse.

E. Anti-dumping laws

In the case of multi-national organisations it should be noted that goods, either in finished or unfinished form, when transferred from a multi-national parent company to a foreign subsidiary are often subject to the customs laws of the foreign country. These customs laws have two purposes:

1. the raising of revenue,
2. the protection of their home industries against the dumping of excess production of the companies of other countries.

There can be little doubt that the method of inter-unit pricing used to place a value on goods transferred between parent and subsidiary companies in other countries has legal implications. Customs tariff laws and anti-dumping laws of Canada, the USA, Mexico and many other countries appear to place a definite requirement on the method of inter-unit pricing between domestic corporations and foreign subsidiaries. For goods with an established market, the fair market value must be used – for all other goods, full manufacturing and distribution costs must be included.

8. Legal implications

It would appear reasonable to assume that there is nothing to prevent a division which sells a product both to other divisions and to outside customers, from using a transfer price which differs from the outside price. Otherwise transactions between divisions would be subject to restrictions not applying to transactions between departments within a division or between departments of a non-divisionalised company.

In the USA the position is less clear when a unit is separately incorporated as a subsidiary company, for the Supreme Court has held that a parent company and its subsidiaries are capable of conspiring together in restraint of trade. In that country it would appear that a corporation which transfers products to its own organisational units at a price lower than it sells to outside purchasers gives itself a discriminatory competitive advantage in the eyes of the law. The inference is that the transfer of produce from a subsidiary to a parent company at a price equal to cost, or in any event less than the market price, could be construed as helping to infringe the US anti-trust laws. However, it should be noted that it would not constitute a violation of anti-trust laws in the absence of other practices which restrict free trade.

9. Conclusion

Investigations carried out in multi-divisional organisations have confirmed a number of the points claimed by writers on the subject. It can be concluded, for example, that the manager of a purchasing division is not concerned with the breakdown of the inter-unit transfer price into its fixed and variable cost elements – the cost to him varies directly according to the number of units bought from the supplying division and is therefore wholly variable from his viewpoint. The amount of the fixed cost included by the supplying division in the transfer price is however dependent on the number of units produced and sold, so that a change in the number of units will have a significant effect on the profitability of the supplying division. This means that the full cost can never be a satisfactory basis for establishing transfer prices because it does not provide a satisfactory guide to decision making and that sub-optimisation may be the outcome if full information relating to the cost of the product transferred is not communicated to the purchaser.

Second, a transfer pricing system based on marginal cost to the supplying division, but not permitting that division to earn a profit, ignores the divisional performance measurement aspect and therefore cannot be employed without the removal of the decision-making autonomy from divisional management. This is because, as long as marginal cost transfer pricing is in operation, the supplying division will not absorb its fixed costs in the transfer price and will show a loss which will adversely affect overall performance so that it will not be employed by divisional managers who are permitted to decide whether or not to trade internally. Similarly, in situations where marginal cost is increasing with volume, marginal cost will vary according to the total demand of the buying division added to the demands of the supplying division's customers.

In these circumstances neither division can make its decisions relating to output independently, so that complete autonomy of the individual division is no longer possible.

Third, because accounting systems do not record the opportunity cost of the best alternative rejected, an important aspect of the transfer pricing problem is sometimes overlooked. Where excess operating capacity can be eliminated by a small decrease in the selling price of the intermediate product to outside buyers, the opportunity cost of selling the intermediate product internally becomes significant and the profits accruing from existing sales of the finished product must be reviewed. Each time the forecast of opportunity cost is changed, the optimal decision relating to the volume of inter-unit trading must be revised.

Then there is the problem of determining the validity of the price at which the intermediate product is available from outside suppliers. Where this price can be interpreted as a distress price, offered by the outside supplier in a desperate bid to retain business in the hope that it can be increased later and that subsequent profits will absorb present losses, it can hardly be a valid basis for a transfer price. Whether or not a price can be termed a distress price must depend on the particular circumstances of each situation, and this may be difficult to determine in some cases, but if it is acknowledged that the price is unlikely to be offered for any length of time in the future, it cannot be a reliable yardstick on which to base an inter-unit transfer price. Where the question of a division ceasing to produce an intermediate product because of the availability of a similar product at a cheaper price on the open market arises, careful consideration must be given to the cost of re-entering this field at a later date, should the outside supplier subsequently raise his price.

In situations where a division is responsible for an error in inter-unit transactions, it is a general principle that the division should be required to pay only when the error results in loss of profits to the organisation as a whole. If a loss of profits to the company has not occurred, the divisions should be placed in the financial position which they would have enjoyed had no mistake occurred. On the other hand, if an incorrect make or buy decision results in the profitability level of the whole company being put in jeopardy, the reduction in profit should be reflected in the profit and loss account of the division responsible for the error.

Finally, it should be appreciated that the existence of a market price arrived at by arms length competitive bargaining between an independent buyer and seller does not always guarantee the best price for the optimum benefit of the organisation as a whole. Transfer prices agreed in these circumstances can motivate divisional managers to take decisions which are not in the company's interests and therefore lead to a lack of goal congruence.

Consideration is given in the Appendix to the strengths and weaknesses of the various pricing methods used to record inter-unit transfers.

10. Summary
It will be appreciated from the foregoing that a number of difficulties have to be overcome by managements who are faced with the problem of establishing an inter-unit transfer pricing mechanism. It seems clear that consideration should always be given to the following points:

1. The opportunity to submit a quotation should always be made available to an internal supplying division when the management of that division believes that it can produce the required product. The onus should be on the buying division to provide facilities to enable the selling division to submit a competitive quotation. In return, as full information as possible relating to the cost structure of the product being traded should be made available to the purchasing division in order that the effect of their decision on the overall profitability of the company may be assessed by the management of that division.

2. Opportunities to re-quote should be made available to the supplying division when its original quotation exceeds the outside competitor's quotation which the buying division is proposing to accept. It should be recognised however that outside suppliers will cease to submit competitive quotations if their quotations are always unsuccessful.

3. Transfer prices for any work should always be agreed in advance of the work being performed.

4. Whilst a market price, or a market equivalent price if it exists, should be the basis of the inter-unit price, the variable and fixed cost elements incurred in the manufacture of the product ought to be considered in relation to this price. In particular it should be recognised that a competitor not operating on a decentralised control basis may have an advantage and due allowance ought therefore to be made. Allowance should also be made for the saving in selling expenses normally incurred in making outside

sales and the absence of collection expenses, credit control and bad debt costs.

5. In the absence of a market equivalent price, a negotiating procedure should be adopted by the trading divisions. These negotiations should not be permitted to become unduly protracted and whilst head office intervention should be restricted to a minimum, arbitration by a representative of central management should be available in those instances where both parties request it. Otherwise, in the interests of autonomy the offer and acceptance procedure should be left to the divisional management on the understanding that both parties are fully informed on the significance of the transaction in relation to the profitability of the company as a whole.

6. Prices based on total costs incurred should never be employed except in situations where the final contract with the outside customer is on a cost-plus basis.

INTER-UNIT TRANSFER PRICING

Appendix – Transfer pricing methods

In this appendix consideration is given first to the various types of cost based prices, then market based prices are examined and the relationship of negotiated prices to the alternative bases is considered.

1. Cost based prices

In a highly centralised organisation it is likely that top management will determine how many units of output will be produced by the production departments and how many units the distribution department should be able to sell at a range of prices. The responsibility of the production managers will be limited to meeting their production targets at an acceptable level of cost, and the sales management to selling their target quantities, again at an acceptable cost level. In such circumstances, inter-departmental or inter-divisional transfers at full cost to the point of transfer are satisfactory for accounting purposes because the need for determining separate departmental or divisional profits is eliminated. Trading at cost must mean that it is not possible to measure the contribution to profit of each unit of the company.

A. Actual costs

Accordingly, the actual cost price, although relatively simple to calculate and traditionally the method used in valuing stock, is of little worth when evaluating the performance of decentralised units or making decisions based on the profitability of these units. Its use is restricted therefore to situations in which the responsibility for profit performance is centralised.

B. Standard costs

Transfers at standard costs are preferable to actual cost transfers because the use of standard costs prevents the selling division from passing on its inefficiencies in the transfer price.

Nevertheless, some of the criticisms raised against transfers at actual manufacturing costs also apply to standard cost transfers. Whilst the supplying division may derive the benefit of favourable variances from standard, and suffer the unfavourable variances, transfers at standard cost do not provide a proper measure of the profit performance of either unit. It has been suggested that there ought to be a mechanism to ensure that the selling division benefits from savings arising from new methods, where practicable – otherwise the division will not be motivated to introduce new methods.

The major defect of both actual costs and standard cost systems as a basis for transfer pricing is that they fail to provide a sound guide to decision making. The manager of a division which receives intermediate products from another division will treat the transfer price as a variable cost of his own operation – therefore he will not buy unless the price that he can receive from the sale of the final product is sufficient to cover the transfer price plus any additional processing and marketing costs which he may incur. The overall effect of the transaction might be to increase total company profit, but the transfer costs will obscure this fact.

2. Market based prices

A competitive market implies the existence of buyers and sellers, each acting in their own interests to establish prices at which goods are exchanged to mutual benefit. Such a market provides incentive to efficient production because excessive costs cannot be passed on to buyers. By pricing inter-unit transfers at competitive prices, this incentive can be introduced into internal operations which would otherwise be largely insulated from external competitive pressures. In addition, competitive market prices should provide reliable measures of divisional income because these prices are established independently, other than by individuals who have an interest in the results.

Simply recording transactions in the books at the market price has the advantage of giving relatively reliable information on the efficiency of profit centres, compared to competitors. However, it ignores the possibility that both profit centres might find it advantageous to transfer at a lower price. This would be the case if the revenue from an increase in volume were greater than the increase in costs. For this reason, such a policy may have to be suspended from time to time.

This, of course, requires a review of the situation by top management and decentralisation with respect to operating decisions is commensurately less complete. The same situation exists to some extent when profit centres, through research, try to estimate what a market price will be. Here again it might be mutually advantageous to trade below the estimated market price. This would be particularly the case if the selling profit centre had lower costs than competitors. It should be noted that there is a mutual advantage in these cases. Therefore, good reasons for an adjustment in the transfer price is more likely to be called to central management's attention and the adjustments more readily agreed upon.

A number of difficulties exist in the practical application of market based transfer prices.

1. Conditions may make published statistics an inaccurate statement of the market price for the size, quality, timing and location of the inter-unit transactions. If market determined price spreads are large, it is likely that they cannot be established objectively in a manner that will be satisfactory to buyer and seller without negotiation.

2. The market place may not offer a real alternative for the inter-unit buyer or seller because of differences in volume or quality standards.

3. It may be difficult to distinguish between nominal price quotations and genuine ones. It has been established in theory that the market price is the most desirable transfer price in situations where the intermediate market is competitive. However, the situation is subject to qualification in many cases in practice. When the market price approach is used, it should be ensured that the transfer of the goods takes place at a price which is no higher than that prevailing in an outside market at the time of the transfer, i.e. at the price that the receiving division would have to pay to outsiders.

Put another way, the market price approach is an attempt to approximate to an arm's length bargained open market price. The usefulness of the market price method is therefore contingent on the availability of dependable market price quotations of other manufacturers, because it is these prices that would have to be taken into account by parties dealing at arm's length at the established competitive price levels.

In many instances an internal price which is lower than the market price can however, be easily justified, particularly:

(a) when large purchases are made, or
(b) when selling costs are less, or
(c) when an advantage is obtained through an exclusive supplies contract.

These situations can lead to the notion of negotiated market price, whereby the cost savings to the company as a whole are split between the selling and buying divisions through the process of bargaining.

In addition, a practical difficulty arises in the use of the market price basis because either:

(a) few markets are perfectly competitive, or
(b) no intermediate market exists for the exact product or service in question.

A quoted price for a product is only strictly comparable if the credit terms, quality grade and delivery terms etc. are precisely the same for both products.

Similarly, isolated price quotations are sometimes temporary distress or dumping prices. These temporary market prices are not applicable for repetitive high volume transactions and they hurt the credibility of market transfer prices. If distress prices exist, should they be used or should a long run average or normal market price be used instead? The decision must depend on subjective judgments regarding the costs and benefits of each alternative. If the distress price is used, the manager of the supplying division will in the short run meet the price as long as it exceeds his additional cost. In the long run, he has to decide whether or not to cease producing this item. There is a danger that he may decide to stop producing the item because it is having an adverse effect on his divisional rate of return and, as a result, the cut in the total industry's supply may lead to higher outside future prices which will probably be disadvantageous to the company as a whole, in the long run.

The existence of a market price arrived at by arm's length competitive bargaining between independent buyers and sellers does not necessarily guarantee the best price with the optimum benefit to the organisation as a whole. Such transfer prices can motivate divisional managers to make decisions which are bad for the company and therefore lead to a lack of goal congruence. In such instances a transfer price based on a market price can be irrelevant, for market price is only really representative of opportunity cost when the intermediate markets are perfectly competitive i.e. where the company's activity in the market, either in buying or selling, has no influence on the market price.

3. Negotiated prices

In view of the objections to market based prices, a refinement on market price consistent with the view that each decentral ised unit is considered an independent unit, which is based on negotiations or bargaining, has been put forward. The necessary condition for profit centre control is the freedom of divisional managers to negotiate competitive prices in arm's length bargaining and to go outside the company if the prices paid by or to other divisional managers are not acceptable to the managers in question.

A division's profits and, for that matter, executive bonuses can be greatly affected by even small differences in the unit prices of transferred products. However, the identification of the selfish interests of divisional managers and the interests of the company as a whole can be maintained by inter-unit pricing which observes the following principles:

1. Prices of all transfers in and out of a profit centre should be determined by negotiation between buyers and sellers.
2. Negotiators should have access to full data on alternative sources and markets and to public and private information about market prices.
3. Buyers and sellers should be completely free to deal outside the company.
4. Negotiators should be fully informed on the significance of the transaction in relation to the profitability of the company as a whole.

It is generally accepted therefore that, if managers are sophisticated and equipped with good accounting data on their operations, a free negotiation system could satisfy the basic criteria, i.e. a transfer price that will not lead to transfers which will reduce the company's profit but will permit and encourage any transfer which increases that profit. Nevertheless, it has to be noted that the principal disadvantage of such an approach is the amount of executive time which is likely to be taken up. It is true that executives' salaries have to be paid anyway but sooner or later increased demands on executive time will lead to more executives. In such instances it is probably a more profitable use of time to pay attention to the outside market.

A further disadvantage is that negotiated prices can distort the profit centre's financial reports, so that the information which top management has for use in capital budgeting, evaluations etc can be misleading. This is especially true if the range of prices which would be advantageous to both profit centres is quite wide.

However, where there is no outside competitive market and transfers take place in amounts which are neither important nor potentially important, it seems clear that negotiation between divisions is the simplest solution. It would seem that negotiated prices tend to settle down at a figure which is based on the standard cost of the transferred product plus a return on the capital deemed to have been used in its production. Since standard cost generally includes fixed overhead, from the theoretical viewpoint, negotiated prices determined in this way are open to the objection already levelled against any transfer pricing method which turns a division's fixed costs into another division's variable costs by including them in a product price. When the volumes transferred are not large or potentially large it would seem that not much harm can be done by this practice.

Where an outside market does exist for the intermediate product the market price can be important in negotiations, because it provides both parties with an alternative. Dissemination of information relating to this outside market should reduce the bargaining range and permit negotiations to take place in an atmosphere which is conducive to producing transfer prices which are fair approximations to opportunity cost. In the absence of an outside market, the bargaining range is likely to be considerably wider because the buying and selling divisions are in the position known to economists as bilateral monopoly, i.e. the market for the intermediate product consists of two firms, one buying and one selling and neither has an outside alternative. The buyer may buy or not buy or, at the extreme, he may equip his division to manufacture the intermediate product. The seller may sell or not sell or, at the extreme, he may equip his division to manufacture the final product. Under these conditions the market price is likely to be indeterminate within a fairly wide range and the relative profit of the two divisions will depend on the bargaining ability of the respective divisional managers.

4. A general rule

In a recent study carried out in USA[1] a general rule has been developed for selecting a transfer pricing technique.

The transfer price (TP) should equal the standard variable cost (SVC) plus the contribution margin per unit given up on the outside sale by the company when a segment sells internally. The contribution margin given up is referred to as the lost contribution margin (LCM). Symbolically, the general rule is TP = SVC + LCM.

The application of this general rule depends on the characteristics of the market faced by the company and the company's management control process. Applications of the general rule are summarised below.

Situation	*Transfer Pricing Technique*
1. Perfectly competitive market. All products sold internally can be sold externally.	SVC+LCM = the prevailing market price.
2. Slightly imperfect competitive market. All products sold internally can be sold externally.	SVC+LCM = the adjusted market price. The adjusted market price is the prevailing market price adjusted for identifiable and quantifiable market imperfections, such as economies from selling internally. If the market faced by the selling division is more than slightly imperfectly competitive, the adjusted market price cannot be used.
3. Perfectly competitive market or slightly imperfectly competitive market. Most products sold externally. Products sold internally do not have a market price. Production capacity used to produce internally sold products can be used to produce externally sold products.	SVC+LCM = phantom market price. Since the products sold internally do not have a market price, a phantom market price is created. The phantom market price is the sum of 1. the standard variable cost per unit of the product sold internally and 2. the contribution margin per unit lost by not producing products that can be sold externally.

[1] 'Transfer Pricing: Techniques and Uses': Benke and Edwards (National Association of Accountants).

Bibliography

Abdel-Khalik, A. Rashad, and Edward J. Lusk. "Transfer Pricing: A Synthesis." *Accounting Review* 69 (January 1974): 8–23.

Agmon, Tamir. *Political Economy and Risk in World Financial Markets* (Lexington, Mass.: Lexington Books, 1985).

Aharoni, Yain, and Clifford Baden, *Business in International Environment* (Boulder, Co.: West-view Press, 1977).

American Accounting Association. "Report of the Committee on International Accounting." *Accounting Review* 48 (1973 Supplement): 121–67.

_____ . "Report of the Committee on International Accounting." *Accounting Review* 49 (1974 Supplement): 251–69.

Arpan, Jeffrey S. *International Intracompany Pricing: Non American Systems and Views* (New York: Praeger Publishers, 1972).

Bailey, Andrew D., Jr., and Warren J. Boe. "Goal and Resource Transfers in the Multigoal Organization," *Accounting Review* 51 (July 1976): 559–73.

Ball, Donald A., and Wendell H. McCulloch, Jr. *International Business*. 2nd ed. (Plano, Tex.: Business Publications, 1985).

Baumal, W. J., and T. Fabian, "Decomposition, Pricing for Decentralization, and External Economies." *Management Science* (1964): 1–32.

Benke, Ralph L., Jr., and James Don Edwards. "Should You Use Transfer Pricing to Create Pseudo Centers?" *Management Accounting* (February 1981): 36–39, 43.

_____ . *Transfer Pricing Techniques and Uses* (New York: National Association of Accountants, 1980).

Bierman, Harold. "ROI as a Measure of Managerial Performance." In *Accounting for Managerial Decision Making*, edited by Don T. Decoster et al. 2nd ed. (Santa Barbara, Calif.: Wiley/Hamilton, 1978).

Burns, Jane O. "How IRS Applies the Intercompany Pricing Rules of Section 482: A Corporate Study." *Journal of Taxation* (May 1980): 308–14.

_____ . "The Multinational Enterprise: U.S. Taxation of Foreign Source Income." In *International Accounting*, edited by H. Peter Holzer and others (New York: Harper and Row Publishers, 1984).

Bursk, Edward C., John Dearden, David F. Hawkins, and Victor M. Longstreet. *Financial Control of Multinational Operations* (New York: Financial Executives Research Foundation, 1971).

Business International Corporation. *Forecasting Foreign Exchange Rates*. Management Monograph 55 (New York: Business International Corporation, 1972).

_____ . *Setting Intercorporate Pricing Policies*. Business International Research Report. (New York: Business International Corporation, 1973).

Choi, Federick D. S. "Global Finance and Accounting Uniformity." *University of Michigan Business Review* (September 1976): 48.

Choi, Frederick D. S., and Gerhard G. Mueller. *International Accounting* (Englewood Cliffs, N.J.: Prentice-Hall, 1984).

_____ . *An Introduction to Multinational Accounting* (Englewood Cliffs, N.J.: Prentice-Hall, 1978).

Clark, John J., Thomas J. Hindelang, and Robert E. Pritchard. *Capital Budgeting: Planning and Control of Capital Expenditures*. 2nd ed. (Englewood Cliffs, N.J.: Prentice-Hall, 1984).

Eccles, Robert G. *The Transfer Pricing Problem: A Theory for Practice* (Lexington, Mass.: Lexington Books, 1985).

Farmer, Richard N., and Barry M. Richman. *International Business* 3rd ed. (Bloomington, Ind.: Cedarwood Press, 1980).

Gordon, Lawrence, A., and George E. Pinches. *Improving Capital Budgeting: A Decision Support System Approach* (Reading, Mass.: Addison-Wesley Publishing Company, 1984).

Greene, James, and Michael G. Duerr. *Inter Company Transactions in the Multinational Firm: A Survey* (National Industrial Conference Board, 1970).

Greenhill, C. R., and E. O. Herbalzheimer. "International Transfer Pricing: The Restructive Business Practices Approach." *Journal of World Trade Law* (May–June 1980): 232–41.

Hall, L. le Van. "The Multinational Corporation: Its Impact on Developing Countries." In *The Multinational Corporation: Accounting and*

Social Implications (Urbana: Center for International Education and Research in Accounting, University of Illinois, 1977).

Helmers, Dag. "BOAC's Response to the OECD Report on Transfer Pricing and Multinational Enterprises." *Intertax* (August 1980): 286–93.

Horngren, Charles T., and George Foster. *Cost Accounting: A Managerial Emphasis*. 6th ed. (Englewood Cliffs, N.J.: Prentice-Hall, 1987).

An Introduction to Financial Control and Reporting in Multinational Enterprise (Austin: Bureau of Business Research, University of Texas at Austin, 1973).

Killius, Juergen. "Foreign Income Business Operations in West Germany." *Tax Management* (1985): A–61.

Kim, H. Seung, and Stephen W. Miller. "Constituents of the International Transfer Pricing Decisions." *Columbia Journal of World Business* (Spring 1979): 69–77.

Knowles, Lynette L., and Ike Mathur. "Factors Influencing the Designing of International Transfer Pricing Systems." *Managerial Finance* 11 (1985): 17–20.

_____ . "International Transfer Pricing Objectives." *Managerial Finance* 11 (1985): 12–16.

Lawler, Edward. *Motivation in Work Organizations*. (Belmont, Calif.: Wadsworth Publishing Company, 1973).

Liebman, Howard M. "International Transfer Pricing and Recent Development: Part I." *Tax Planning International Review* (August 1987): 4–7.

Maciariello, Joseph A. *Management Control Systems* (Englewood Cliffs, N.J.: Prentice-Hall, 1984).

Malmstrom, Duane. "Accommodating Exchange Rate Fluctuations in Intercompany Pricing and Invoicing." *Management Accounting* (September 1977): 24–28.

Mason, R. Hal, Robert R. Miller, and Dale R. Weigel. *International Business*. 2nd ed. (New York: John Wiley and Sons, 1981).

Mueller, Gerhard G., Helen Gernon, and Gary Meek. *Accounting: An International Perspective* (Homewood, Ill.: Richard D. Irwin, 1987).

Nagy, Richard J. "Transfer Price Accounting for MNEs." *Management Accounting* (January 1978): 34–38.

Organization for Economic Cooperation and Development. Committee on Fiscal Affairs. *Transfer Pricing and Multinational Enterprises* (Paris: Organization for Economic Cooperation and Development, 1979).

Otley, D. T., and A. J. Berry. "Control, Organization, and Accounting." In *Reading in Cost Accounting, Budgeting, and Control*, edited by William E. Thomas, 6th ed. (Cincinnati: South Western Publishing Co., 1983).

Oxelheim, Lars. *International Financial Market Fluctuations*. (New York: John Wiley and Sons, 1985).

Persen, William, and Van Lessig. *Evaluating the Financial Performance of Overseas Operations* (New York: Financial Executive Research Foundation, 1978).

Plosschaert, Sylvain R. F. "The Multiple Motivations for Transfer Pricing Modulations in Multinational Enterprises and Governmental Counter Measures: An Attempt at Clarification." *Management International Review* (1981/1): 49–63.

_____ . *Transfer Pricing and Multinational Corporations: An Overview of Concepts, Mechanisms, and Regulations* (New York: Praeger Publishers, 1979).

Robbins, Sidney M., and Robert B. Stobaugh. "The Bent Measuing Stick for Foreign Subsidiaries." *Harvard Business Review* (September–October 1973): 80–88.

_____ . *Money in the Multinational Enterprise* (New York: Basic Books, 1973).

Robock Stefan H., and Kenneth Simmonds, *International Business and Multinational Enterprises*. 3rd ed. (Homewood, Ill.: Richard D. Irwin, 1983).

Ronen, Joshua, and George McKinney. "Transfer Pricing for Divisional Autonomy." *Journal of Accounting Research* 8 (Spring 1970): 99–110.

Rugman, Alan M. "Internationalization Theory and Corporate International Finance." *California Management Review* (Winter 1980): 73–79.

Rugman, Alan M., and Lorraine Eden. "Introduction." In *Multinationals and Transfer Pricing* (New York: Saint Martin's Press, 1985).

Schindler, Guenter. "Intercompany Transfer Pricing after Tax Reform of 1986." *Tax Planning International Review* (November 1987): 9–10.

Scott, George M. "Planning, Control, and Performance Evaluation Systems in International Operations." *Cost and Management* (Canada) (January–February 1977): 4–9.

Shapiro, Alan. *Multinational Financial Management* (Boston: Allyn and Bacon, 1986).

Solomons, David. *Divisional Performance: Measurement and Control* (Homewood, Ill.: Richard D. Irwin, 1965).

Stonehill, Arthur, and Leonard Nathanson. "Capital Budgeting and the Multinational Corporation." *California Management Review* (Summer 1968): 39–54.

Symons, Terry, and Richard Harris. "International Transfer Pricing: Revenue Authorities Put Multinational Business on the Alert." *Tax Planning International Review* (December 1987): 7–11.

Tang, Roger Y. W. *Multinational Transfer Pricing: Canadian and British Perspectives.* (Toronto, Canada: Butterworth and Co., 1981).

Tang, Roger Y. W., C. K. Walter, and Robert H. Raymond. "Transfer Pricing—Japanese vs. American Style." *Management Accounting* (January 1979): 12-16.

Wu, Frederick H., and Douglas Sharp. "An Empirical Study of Transfer Pricing Practice." *International Journal of Accounting, Education, and Research* 14 (Spring 1979): 71-99.

Yunker, Penelope J. "A Survey Study of Subsidiary Autonomy, Performance Evaluation and Transfer Pricing in Multinational Corporations." *Columbia Journal of World Business* (Fall 1983): 51-64.

Index

About the Author

WAGDY M. ABDALLAH is Associate Professor of Accounting at Seton Hall University and a member of the American Accounting Association's Committee on International Accounting.